# A COMPREHENSIVE GUIDE TO SUICIDAL BEHAVIOURS

# A COMPREHENSIVE GUIDE TO SUICIDAL BEHAVIOURS

*Working with Individuals at Risk of Suicide and their Families*

David Aldridge and Sergio Pérez Barrero

Jessica Kingsley *Publishers*
London and Philadelphia

First published in 2012
by Jessica Kingsley Publishers
116 Pentonville Road
London N1 9JB, UK
and
400 Market Street, Suite 400
Philadelphia, PA 19106, USA

*www.jkp.com*

**Library of Congress Cataloging in Publication Data**
Aldridge, David, 1947-
  A comprehensive guide to suicidal behaviours : working with individuals at risk and their families / David Aldridge and Sergio Pérez Barrero.
       p. ; cm.
  Includes bibliographical references.
  ISBN 978-1-84905-025-8 (alk. paper)
  I. Pérez Barrero, Sergio Andrés, 1953- II. Title.
  [DNLM: 1. Suicide--prevention & control. 2. Crisis Intervention. 3. Professional-Family Relations. 4. Risk Management. 5. Suicidal Ideation. WM 165]

   362.28--dc23

                    2011046689

**British Library Cataloguing in Publication Data**
A CIP catalogue record for this book is available from the British Library

ISBN 978 1 84905 025 8
eISBN 978 0 85700 515 1

Printed and bound in Great Britain

*To Max, Morella, Lauren and Sergio*

# ACKNOWLEDGEMENT

Thank you to David del Llano Sosa for the original translation of Professor Pérez Barrero's manuscript into English.

# CONTENTS

NOTE ON VOCABULARY............................................. 9

**Chapter 1**
Introduction: The Individual in a Process of Escalating
Distress........................................... 11

**Chapter 2**
Suicidal Behaviour in a Historical Context........... 19

**Chapter 3**
Classifications of Suicide.......................... 37

**Chapter 4**
Myths about Suicide............................ 49

**Chapter 5**
Talking about Suicidal Ideas ...................... 57

**Chapter 6**
Suicide Risk Groups ........................... 63

**Chapter 7**
Protective Factors in Suicidal Behaviour ........... 79

**Chapter 8**
Family Problems ................................ 85

**Chapter 9**
The Survivor and Complicated Grief............... 97

**Chapter 10**
Psychotherapy for Suicidal People in Crisis .......... 105

## Chapter 11

The Internet: New Possibilities, Problems and Challenges
in the Prevention of Suicide . . . . . . . . . . . . . . . . . . . . . .   137

## Chapter 12

Recommendations for a Suicide Prevention Strategy . .   145

APPENDIX 1: A MODEL OF THE SYSTEMIC MANAGEMENT OF DISTRESS .   155

APPENDIX 2: GLOSSARY OF TERMS . . . . . . . . . . . . . . . . . . . . . . . . . . . . .   161

REFERENCES . . . . . . . . . . . . . . . . . . . . . . . . . . . . . . . . . . . . . . . . . . . .   181

FURTHER INFORMATION. . . . . . . . . . . . . . . . . . . . . . . . . . . . . . . . . . . .   183

INDEX  . . . . . . . . . . . . . . . . . . . . . . . . . . . . . . . . . . . . . . . . . . . . . . . .   185

## List of Figures

1.1    CHANGE, ATTEMPTED SOLUTIONS AND CYCLES OF ESCALATING
       AND DE-ESCALATING DISTRESS IN THE ALDRIDGE MODEL . . . . . .    14

A.1    LEVELS OF ESCALATING DISTRESS AND SYSTEMIC STRATEGIES OF
       MANAGEMENT. . . . . . . . . . . . . . . . . . . . . . . . . . . . . . . . . . . . . . .   157

## List of Tables

2.1    CONTRAST BETWEEN INDIVIDUAL SUICIDES AND SUICIDE
       BOMBERS . . . . . . . . . . . . . . . . . . . . . . . . . . . . . . . . . . . . . . . . . .    35

6.1    RISK FACTORS ASSOCIATED WITH SUICIDE. . . . . . . . . . . . . . . . . . .    76

7.1    PROTECTIVE FACTORS ASSOCIATED WITH SUICIDE . . . . . . . . . . . .    80

9.1    SIGNS AND SYMPTOMS THAT MAY OCCUR IN COMPLICATED
       GRIEF. . . . . . . . . . . . . . . . . . . . . . . . . . . . . . . . . . . . . . . . . . . . . .   102

10.1   STAGES OF PSYCHOLOGICAL FIRST AID . . . . . . . . . . . . . . . . . . . . .   115

10.2   DIFFERING THERAPEUTIC RELATIONSHIPS ACCORDING TO
       PERCEIVED PERSONAL RESPONSIBILITY IN THE PÉREZ BARRERO
       APPROACH. . . . . . . . . . . . . . . . . . . . . . . . . . . . . . . . . . . . . . . . . .   128

# NOTE ON VOCABULARY

For ease of reading we alternate the use of male and female pronouns throughout the book.

## Chapter 1

# INTRODUCTION

## The Individual in a Process
## of Escalating Distress

The World Health Organization highlights the fact that all cultures are affected by suicide and says that strategies for prevention should take this dimension of culture into account. Almost a million people commit suicide every year, which is about 1.8 per cent of the total burden of disease worldwide.[1] From these statistics we can estimate that a loved one is lost to suicide every 40 seconds. In all regions of the world, this poses a tragic loss of life.

Every year suicide yields more deaths than traffic accidents and if suicide were recognized as a disease, then we could say we had reached epidemic proportions in some parts of the world. We have seen an increase in suicides in the last 45 years and there is an increase in suicide in young people, causing continuing concern.

In most recent armed conflicts, casualties have amounted to thousands, tens of thousands, hundreds of thousands, but rarely to millions. However, it is not war but people killing themselves that is causing concern. With a million suicides and between ten and twenty million suicide attempts annually, we have a massive problem worldwide.

---

1   These statistics and more can be found at the World Health Organization website (www.who.int/mental_health/prevention/suicide/suicideprevent/en).

Although definitive causes of suicide remain unknown to date, we know that there are general problems that are major risk factors. These include mental disorders, depression and alcohol abuse in the Western world. A general platitude is that the problem is complex, but this does not mean that we should not try to find a way to avoid young people killing themselves. One of the problems is that we often try to find singular approaches, as if there were a pill to make us happy. In this book we focus on an interdisciplinary approach that looks at the individual, at the family and personal relationships they have and at the communities in which they are embedded. Sometimes, it is the lack of community ties and personal relationships that is the very ground in which personal despair flourishes.

It is impossible to know for sure who will commit suicide, but major suicide risk groups have been identified. Among them are depressed people, people who have attempted suicide, who have threatened to commit suicide or have a suicidal plan, relatives of a person who has completed suicide and vulnerable people in crisis situations. Our position is that that the motives for suicide can be grouped into two categories in most countries, despite their cultural differences. These categories are spousal conflicts and familial conflicts. An overarching concept underlying this is that these conflicts occur at times of change in a relationship and one person becomes identified as the 'wrongdoer' or the 'deviant' person. It is often this person who has had a history of being the 'sick' person in the family and is increasingly seen in a negative light. It is the individual who becomes suicidal, but the context for that suicide is relational. This is not to deny that such conflicts occur when people face massive financial challenges.

Suicide is the final symptom of an unhappy existence. It can also be considered 'a chronicle of an announced death', paraphrasing the words of Colombian novelist and short-story writer Gabriel García Márquez. Everyone knows that a suicidal person will eventually die by suicide since they may have hinted what is coming in some way. However, a suicidal message is often neither decoded nor taken seriously by their immediate family. This type of communication can be an attempt to inform other people that the person is at the limit of their endurance.

Suicide is a familial problem because it is in the family that most suicides take place. Although primary health physicians are physically very close to suicide, they are still distant from this phenomenon even though they may have seen the person who has committed suicide shortly before the event. Similarly, psychiatrists and psychologists, who may have contact with the person, are even farther from the daily lives of those who wish to commit suicide. Some voluntary social workers, or Samaritans, are as close as family doctors, but they are still distant from the day-to-day existence of the suicide.

Who is closest to the person committing suicide then? Undoubtedly the family, or those significant others in a person's life who provide a community of intimates. That is why we recommend that suicide prevention begins and ends in the family, even though we know that the majority of suicides occur in families whose members do not understand the signs of a suicidal crisis in one of its members. Indeed, one of the problems may be that a family member has become estranged and an 'outsider'.

What should the family know? The family should familiarize themselves with the different manifestations of suicidal communication and learn to ask life-saving questions fearlessly; that is, questions that explore the presence of suicidal thoughts.

The main aim of the present book is to enable the family, and everyone else interested in preventing this cause of death, to keep the suicidal person alive until they have access to professional help and to cooperate actively with that help. For those people working in situations that are not primarily family orientated, we can substitute the concepts of significant others or a community of intimates; that is, people who have some connection to the distressed person in their daily lives.

## THE ALDRIDGE MODEL OF DISTRESS

Suicidal behaviour is complex. Yet, when we take a relational perspective on the problem, we see a simple, repeated pattern of ever-escalating cycles of distress (see Figure 1.1). People attempt to resolve their distress. However, that distress escalates. Instead of being resolved in the ways we expect, things get worse. Sometimes, the way that we try to resolve distress has the opposite effect. It makes things worse. This is compounded even more by the fact that the person attempting to solve the problem becomes seen as deviant and as causing the problem. No matter what they try to do, they are seen as being in the wrong. The consequence is that that person becomes isolated. In addition, that person sees the people trying to help them as misguided or failing to help. This erodes the helping relationship and brings about the pattern we see of people becoming more and more distressed, moving from one helper to another, forever seeking more specialist care.

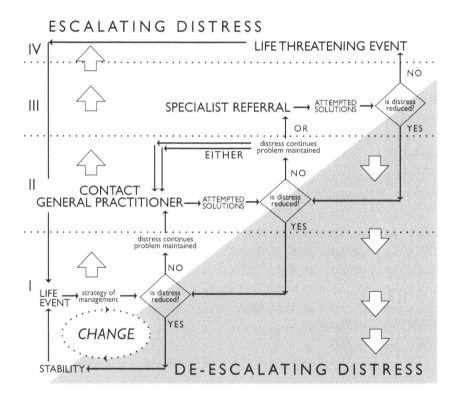

Figure 1.1 Change, attempted solutions and cycles of escalating and de-escalating distress in the Aldridge model[2]

2    From Aldridge, D. (1998) *Suicide: The Tragedy of Hopelessness.* London: Jessica Kingsley Publishers.

We see how, in Figure 1.1, a person tries to solve her problems herself (Level I). This fails and she then contacts her general practitioner, who may prescribe medication (Level II). This may work for a short time, but if her problems remain distressing she will be referred to more specialist help (Level III). When specialist help also provides no lasting solution, and distress prevails, then we often see an episode of life-threatening behaviour (Level IV). Of course, it is possible at any stage to intervene and resolve distress. The main point is that the source of her distress must be recognized, confronted and resolved. As we will see later, the source of this distress may lie in a deteriorating personal relationship, and it is a relational solution that is necessary. We are not denying that there is personal psychological distress and emotional difficulty, but this personal suffering is embedded within a nexus of relational difficulties, a social milieu and a cultural context. Personal solutions will not solve continuing relational problems.

We know that many completed suicides are preceded by attempted suicides. Many of these are blamed upon deteriorating personal relationships. Change in family systems must be adapted to (see Figure 1.1). People leave a family through death, divorce or separation. Someone new may come into the family. These life events are challenging. How those challenges are met and accommodated is not simply the responsibility of one family member, but it may be one family member who appears to be voicing the collective distress of a family. Some people abuse medication, intended to be helpful in the short term, to resolve their distress. Others may use alcohol as a way of coping with loss or challenging events. However, these attempted solutions become part of a strategy of distress management that fails. The source of that distress remains and is located within the ecology of people living their lives together, although expressed by one person. The tragedy is that the ways of trying to resolve distress may cause more personal suffering, if the underlying cause is not discovered. Using alcohol to solve a relational problem may become a 'drink' problem for the individual. The use of pain medication to relieve suffering may become a substance-abuse problem when the pain is related to the emotional distress of a difficult relationship.

Using anxiety-reducing pills for panic attacks, when the basis for the distress is a marital conflict, is ignoring the source of that problem.

However, if we look at this in terms of family process, then we can also see ways of bringing about change to resolve that distress. We can redefine what appear as maladaptive, delinquent acts into attempts at problem resolution. Rather than look at the personal inadequacies of those involved, we look at what has happened in terms of their family significance. We can also look to the competencies that people have. There may indeed be conflict, but we look at positive ways of conflict resolution that attempt to discover the underlying and unresolved problem.

The shift in focus here, of taking a relational perspective and seeing what positive resources people have, has further implications, mainly on the goal of therapy. Therapy does not seek to fix what went wrong or to accommodate pathology and deviance – it enables the beginning of a process of change by referring to competence and resources. The efforts of all participants join to negotiate the same means and attain the same goal, which is to relieve distress. The therapist plays the role of a facilitator, offering choices and making them available to the family. We refer here to a repertoire of distress management. We all have a repertoire of behavioural responses at times of difficulty: confront the problem; withdraw from the problem; talk to a friend; see a counsellor; ask your general practitioner; use prescription medication; look for advice on the internet; or have a drink, pray for guidance and hope the problem goes away. We learn these repertoires in our families, in the institutions where we learn or work, and from the cultures in which we take part. All of these are valid when they work. When distress is not resolved, then we need a broader repertoire of solutions.

How we respond to challenges and distress is a dynamic process that occurs over time and is multi-faceted. The approaches that we take to resolving distress must also be multi-faceted; that is, we extend our repertoire of distress management. We can do this personally, but also with our friends and family, and socially with the helping agencies in our communities.

The wider perspective of this approach has its focus not only on the individual, and his or her behaviour, but on the whole complex of significant others and the different systems in which he or she operates. We live in close relationships that are located within the larger context of community. These communities also offer us resources that we can draw upon when distressed.

What is essential for any positive change to relieve distress is a flexible repertoire of distress management. The problem with suicidal behaviour itself is that it is a 'one size fits all' solution and as such is a limited repertoire of distress management that itself prolongs suffering.

# CHAPTER 2

# SUICIDAL BEHAVIOUR IN A HISTORICAL CONTEXT

Suicide is as old as mankind. A poem from the Middle Kingdom of Egypt (ca 2055–1650 BC) describes the struggle of a suicide with his self-destructive impulses:

> Death is before me today:
>> like the recovery of a sick man,
>> like going forth into a garden after sickness.
> Death is before me today:
>> like the odour of myrrh,
>> like sitting under a sail in a good wind.
> Death is before me today:
>> like the course of a stream;
>> like the return of a man from the war-galley to his house.
> Death is before me today:
>> like the home that a man longs to see,
>> after years spent as a captive.[1]

Yet this poem is not simply about suicide but confronts death itself. It is this confrontation with death, and willingness to talk about it, that is important. In talking about death, we are turned also towards

---

1   The poem and background information can be found at www.consolatio. com/2009/06/ancient-egyptian-death-is-before-me-today.html.

the meaning and value of life. For many of the people we see who are suicidal, it is the meaning of their life that is being questioned. Paradoxically, what is a concern with how to live differently may be stated as wanting to die or a longing for death.

The whole assisted suicide debate revolves around this longing for death at a time when life is potentially intolerable. When palliative care is unavailable, or fails, then people turn to resolving their death by asking someone to help them die. Similarly, the thought of intolerable suffering in the future encourages some people to contemplate death when a foreseen physical or mental status occurs.

When this is discussed, it often comes under the heading 'end of life decisions'. In some countries – Belgium, the Netherlands, some states in the United States of America (Washington, Oregon and Montana), Sweden, Switzerland and Australia – doctor-assisted suicide is legal. In these countries, there have been special considerations about the nature of unbearable suffering, the patient being 'tired of life' and no longer having the will to live. In addition, patients expect a loss of control over their lives and a debilitated future.

Some people refer to the Henry Fielding statement that it is not death but dying which is terrible, and this has raised discussions about a good quality of death. Most scientific work on death applies to death from cancer in hospices, and this is different from the experience of death in geriatric wards. The general medical recommendations are that patients should be free from symptoms like pain and anxiety; that death should occur in familiar surroundings and that relatives should be aware that the patient is dying and be present if desired. 'Dying well' is literally the English meaning of euthanasia: from the Greek *eu*, 'well' + *thanatos*, 'death'.

We see here that in the special circumstances of modern life, death may be contemplated. What lies behind this thinking reflects that as human beings we have always contemplated our own mortality and the meaning of life. Indeed, in previous centuries and in some current situations, there are times when existence itself is threatened. How we contemplate survival and suffering and then cope with existential challenges requires a repertoire of coping mechanisms, what we refer to here as 'a repertoire of distress management'. Further than that, we also need a cognitive repertoire for contemplating the meaning of our lives and a vocabulary for discussing both life and death.

## SUICIDE THROUGHOUT HISTORY

Outbreaks of suicide throughout history, as today, were causes for concern. Throughout the seventeenth century, the causes of suicide were seen as sickness of mind, intemperance, gluttony, duelling and foolhardiness. A century later, causal factors became related to the environment, such as polluted air, poor diet and idleness, which heralded a change from a moral to a secular view of suicidal behaviour. The very circumstance of living in unhealthy cities was blamed for the 'English malady' of suicide. So prevalent was suicide in the eighteenth century that it was considered as a problem constituting a national emergency. Such a concern is echoed today.

In eighteenth-century Geneva there was a rapid increase in suicides. The availability of firearms appears to have been a contributory factor, echoing familiar concerns today in developing countries. Economic problems played their part as the watch-making industry declined. While foreigners and the poor were over-represented amongst suicides, the well-to-do were also prone to taking their own lives. Concurrently, suicide was decriminalized, the judicial authorities no longer confiscated the property of suicides, and funeral rites were no longer denied to them.

Changing attitudes towards courtship, marriage and the family in eighteenth-century Geneva contributed to this dramatic increase in the suicide rate. Unprecedented numbers of people took their lives because of marital breakdown or unhappy love stories, and in response to the deaths of family members. After 1750, marriage appeared to offer immunity to suicide for both men and women. As today, those who lived alone were at risk, particularly the widowed. Marriage appears to have protected against suicidal feelings, in that people were investing themselves emotionally in a marital relationship, yet some suicides were perceived as being motivated by relational causes: loss of a loved one, domestic disputes and romantic misadventures. Later in the century, however, suicides were attributed to unrequited love, love affairs that went awry or marital conflict. The change to a companionate marriage, from that of a marriage of convenience, brought new expectations of personal happiness within a romantic marital relationship. With marital dissatisfaction, and failed expectations, came conflict and divorce. Generational conflicts between adolescents and their parents made themselves apparent. Again we see a current concern about relationships within families reflected in the past. As the family became more of a focus for emotions, then grief at the loss of a family member became another attributed motivation for suicide.

As we see through the ages, and as today, marriage or a stable relationship appears to protect against suicide. However, when a relationship breaks down, there is distress.

Throughout history, death was actively contemplated, and suicide was seen as a legitimate form of death if the grounds for that suicide were present. These grounds depended upon both time and culture. As we will see below, suicide has also been depicted in mythology and the arts as being a serious subject for contemplation regarding the human condition. The Greek philosophers took suicide as a legitimate act, and since then painters throughout the centuries have taken suicide as a dramatic focus for their paintings. We have, then, a topic that is built into the historical fabric of Western cultures and thereby indirectly legitimized as a subject of contemplation.

In Ancient Mexico, the Mayan goddess Ixtab was the protector of those who committed suicide, a common way of death among the indigenous population in that country. This goddess is depicted with a rope around her neck and signs of putrefaction on her face. In this case, suicide by hanging was considered an honourable way to die. Ixtab would accompany such suicides to paradise where the dead person would be joined by slain warriors, sacrificial victims, priests and women who died in childbirth. In paradise, they would all be rewarded with delicious food and drink, resting under the shade of a pleasant tree, free from all want. We also see this reflected in the attitude of suicide bombers as being martyrs for a cause and gaining their rewards in paradise.

For many cultures, suicide was concerned with saving face or maintaining honour. In the Eastern world, suicide was considered a legitimate or indifferent act and in Ancient Japan, *hara-kiri* and *seppuku* are described as traditional methods of suicide used by men who had lost their honour. To continue living meant a disgrace for them and their families.

In the Louvre Museum in Paris, there is a Corinthian seal dating from 700 BC that represents the death of Ajax, the son of Telamon, run through by his own sword, the method chosen by him to commit suicide. The story goes that Ajax kills himself rather than live in shame. He believes himself to be the rightful recipient of magical armour because of his strength and courage and the fighting that he has done for the Greeks. Instead, the armour is given to the better orator, Odysseus. This too is a common theme in suicide where people consider themselves to have been wronged by their families or friends or the people they have worked with; they either wreak their revenge by killing themselves or cannot cope with what they perceive to be the shame of not being recognized for their value.

Hannibal, the famous military leader, led his forces, including elephants, across the Alps and into Rome, where he terrorized Roman forces. He had waged victorious campaigns across Spain before eventually marching on Rome. Despite early success, he found it difficult to maintain control and was forced to withdraw and negotiate peace. Failing to recapture his earlier military glory, he ended up taking his own life by swallowing poison. Unable to accommodate a new identity, he kills himself. One feature of some suicides is that the person refuses to accept a new identity; rather than face change, they can only accept their previous identity. This identity may be violated through shame, or being no longer 'glorious' and, finding this unacceptable, the person chooses death rather than a changed identity.

In 410 BC, Amicus painted Canace's death. She was lying dressed in a tunic with a dagger in her hand. She was forced by her father to commit suicide as punishment for falling in love with her brother Macareus. Although it is Canace who dies, she is forced into this within a family context of shame. This familial context is relevant today when we consider how people become suicidal.

There are many cases of famous people in history who died by suicide. The Roman philosopher Seneca acted for a while as Nero's adviser. However, he lost his influence over Nero so he retired and devoted his time to study and writing. Later, Seneca was caught up in the aftermath of a plot to kill Nero and was ordered by Nero to kill himself. To do this, he followed a Roman tradition by severing several veins and immersing himself in a warm bath so that he would bleed to death. His wife Pompeia also attempted to kill herself at this time. This method of suicide, exsanguination, is still used today.

A wife killing herself after the death of a spouse is also a part of the story of Cleopatra. With Cleopatra the familial and relational story is, like all suicides, complex. Mark Anthony spends the winter in Alexandria and eventually leaves to carry on his duties as the ruler of the Roman Empire. Six months after his departure, Cleopatra gives birth to their twin sons. Meanwhile, back home, Mark Anthony marries Octavia. Later, however, on a military campaign, he meets up with Cleopatra again, marries her and settles down with her in Alexandria where they have a son together. His first wife, Octavia, tries to arrange a meeting with him but Cleopatra intervenes and the meeting is called off. Eventually, Octavia convinces the Roman senate to declare war on Egypt. In a sea battle, Cleopatra's fleet begins to lose the battle. She flees and Mark Anthony follows her back to Alexandria. Mark Anthony's cavalry desert him and his troops are defeated. He believes that Cleopatra has betrayed him, and she thinks he will harm her and orders her servants to say that she is dead. Believing this to be so, he says that his only reason for living, Cleopatra, has gone and stabs himself in the stomach. After the suicide of Mark Anthony, Cleopatra eventually kills herself by means of an asp bite while being a prisoner of Octavia.

While suicide is often described as an individual act, it is located in literary writing within a set of emotional relationships of lost love and betrayal that are increasingly distressing, sometimes a consequence of shame brought on the family and as a political act where factions take sides against each other.

Lucretia stabbed herself after being raped by Tarquinius. The soldiers, Tarquinius, Collatinus and Junius, were drinking together in a camp outside Rome. A group of soldiers had ridden home unexpectedly the night before to check on their wives. All of their wives were caught betraying their husbands, except for Collatinus' wife, Lucretia. Of the drinking trio, Tarquinius, the king's son, is goaded into testing Lucretia's chastity himself, so he rides to the house where Lucretia is living. Because Tarquinius is a friend of her husband, she is obliged to offer him hospitality and shelter for the night. Later, while Lucretia is sleeping, Tarquinius creeps into her bedroom and rapes her. In the morning, she sends a messenger asking her husband, Collatinus, and her father to come home. She tells them both what has happened. Although both husband and father absolve her of any blame, she feels that she will never be clean again and cannot live with the shame. She kills herself. Although absolved of blame, the distress of the shame she feels overwhelms her.

Shame and honour are interlinked themes as causes for suicide. People want to maintain their cherished identities. Once these identities are violated by events that are out of the hands of the individual, the person may decide to die rather than live with what is, for them, a defiled identity. They would rather be remembered for what they were than for what has become of them.

Demosthenes chose to poison himself after being exiled following a scandal. Rather than fall under the control of those he thought were his enemies, he poisoned himself. Socrates chose the poison hemlock to end his life rather than give up philosophical ideas that were politically incorrect in the view of the government in Athens. Indeed, in the Roman world, suicide was an honourable resolution to a problem for noblemen and noblewomen (not for slaves) until too many noblemen died. Over time, attitudes to suicide have changed – from positive tolerance in certain situations, to condemnation of a forbidden act, to approval when prescribed by a court as an alternative punishment, to regarding it as an act legitimized in certain circumstances and places when supervised by medical practitioners in the case of assisted suicide and euthanasia.

# SUICIDE IN THE BIBLE

Reinforcing the cultural standpoint of suicide in the classical literature, we also read of it in the Old and the New Testaments of the Bible, where several suicides are mentioned. Painters throughout the ages have taken these suicides as subject matter for their work and these are exhibited throughout European art galleries.

The first biblical suicide is Abimelech's (Judges 9:52–55):

> *Abimelech went to the tower and stormed it. But as he approached the entrance to the tower to set it on fire, a woman dropped a millstone on his head and cracked his skull. Hurriedly he called his armour-bearer and said, 'Draw your sword and kill me, so that they can't say, "woman killed him".' So his servant ran him through and he died.*

Abimelech is the first recorded case of euthanasia. The servant killed his master, as commanded, to escape the reputation that his master would have if it were known he had been killed by a woman.

The second case of suicide recorded in the Bible is Samson's (Judges 16:30) death. He prayed to the Lord to be strengthened just once more to get revenge on the Philistines for having been blinded by them. In that moment Samson said:

> *'Let me die with the Philistines!' Then he pushed with all his might and down came the temple on the rulers and all the people in it. Thus he killed many more when he died than while he lived.*

This episode describes both a suicide and an extended homicide. With his own death Samson also killed other people who did not wish to die. We see this today in the acts of both suicide bombers who die for a cause and kill bystanders, and in school slaying where young men who have been bullied shoot their classmates and then kill themselves.

Two other suicides described in the Bible are those of Saul and his armour-bearer (1 Samuel 31:4–5):

> *Saul said to his armour-bearer, 'Draw your sword and run me through or these uncircumcised fellows will come and run me through and abuse me.' But his armour-bearer was terrified and would not do it, so Saul took his own sword and fell on it. When the armour-bearer saw that Saul was dead, he too fell on his sword and died with him.*

The fifth suicide described in the biblical texts is Ahithophel's (2 Samuel 17:23). Ahithophel was a privy councillor whose words were considered divine by both David and David's son, Absalom. When Absalom rebelled against his father, Ahithophel supported him as he thought that he could benefit himself. However, Absalom refused to follow his advice, and when Ahithophel saw that his advice had not been followed, he saddled his donkey and set out for his house in his hometown. He had 'put his house in order', and hanged himself. The description of this event is interesting because it depicts Ahithophel's feelings of uselessness and because 'putting things in order' is also a well-demonstrated sign of an individual contemplating suicide. Hanging has been a prominent method of suicide throughout the ages. But more than this, we see how there is a broader milieu of betrayal and family discord, father being pitted against son.

David could not understand why Ahithophel betrayed him after so many years of faithful service and why he had advised Absalom to let his rebel army try to kill his own father. Even more than this, Ahithophel had urged Absalom to have sexual relationships with his father's concubines in his father's harem on the top of the king's house (2 Samuel 16:20–22). So why does a loyal adviser turn against his king? The reason probably lies in the previous biblical events where David has an adulterous relationship with Bathsheba, getting her pregnant, and ordering the death of her husband. Ahithophel was the grandfather of Bathsheba and would have been publically humiliated. If he had risen up in anger, he too would have been killed. It appears that Ahithophel had waited for revenge until Absalom rebelled against David. He advised him to have sex with all of David's concubines on the roof, just as David had done before with Bathsheba. Revenge is a strong motive and ends in suicide.

The sixth suicide presented in the sacred book is Zimri's (1 Kings 16:18): 'When Zimri saw that the city was taken, he went into the citadel of the royal palace and set the palace on fire around him and he died.' Zimri killed his master Elah, and all his sons, declaring himself king, but his reign only lasted seven days. His army appointed themselves a new leader and they attacked the city where Zimri was living.

Fire or immolation is a highly lethal method that is still widely used in Cuba, particularly in the Eastern part of the country, as well as in Sri Lanka. Repetitions of suicidal attempts using this method are very rare, even in individuals who have suffered monstrous deformations. For centuries, in India, suicide was compulsory for some widows of certain Brahman and royal families. They had to die in their husbands' funeral piles. This custom was called *suttee* and it was declared illegal in 1892. There were earlier practices of immolation in India where relatives or friends could commit suicide at a funeral as a sign of loyalty.

Eleazar was the seventh biblical suicide (1 Maccabees 6:43–46). Like Samson, he died by crushing. While Samson did it for revenge, Eleazar killed himself as an act of altruism. He wanted to end the misery of his people, and possibly wanted to make a name for himself. He crept through the enemy lines under the elephant and speared it from beneath. The biblical description says:

> *And he sacrificed himself to save his people and gain an everlasting fame... When the elephant came he slipped beneath it and gave the animal a deadly strike on his belly. When the elephant fell down, it crushed him and he died right there.*

The eighth suicide described in the Bible is that of Ptolemy Macron (2 Maccabees 10:10–13). He was continuously accused of being a traitor after leaving the Island of Cyprus, which had been confided to him by Philometor, to join Antiochus Epiphanes' party as governor of Coele-Syria and Phenicia. Not being able to fulfil such a huge task decently, and also being accused of treating the Jews kindly and adopting pro-Jewish policies, he felt desperate and decided to end his life by poisoning himself. Substance ingestion appeared as a suicidal method for the first time and this is also the first *soft* or *non-violent* method described, since the rest of the methods mentioned can be considered *hard* or *violent*. The poor self-esteem stemming from the traitor epithet may have contributed to Macron's fatal end but was also confounded by changes in the government at the time and he may have been 'persuaded' to take his own life.

The ninth suicide mentioned in the Bible is that of Razis (2 Maccabees 14:37–46). Like the suicide of Ptolemy Macron, it has a political subtext. Razis was one of the elders of Jerusalem, a patriot with an excellent reputation who was called 'the father of the Jewish nation'. He was denounced to the governor of Judea, Nicanor. Nicanor had been in command of the king's elephants before he became the governor of Judea as appointed by the king, Demetrius. All the Gentiles in Judea supported Nicanor, thinking that the calamities suffered by the Jews would bring prosperity to themselves and were to their advantage. The Jews were thought to be seditious and working against a tranquil united kingdom, so Nicanor was sent out to kill Judas, one of the Jewish leaders, to promote peace. However, Nicanor was impressed by the valour of Judas and how he was fighting for his country, so he negotiated a peace treaty between the two factions instead of fighting further.

The ensuing goodwill between the two purported enemies developed into a close friendship and Judas settled down into a peaceful life. Unfortunately, this companionship between the former enemies fostered jealousy in some quarters and their peace treaty was seen as evidence of disloyalty to the government. The king then wanted Judas to be imprisoned and exiled in Syria. Judas fled, and Nicanor had to seek out a scapegoat to show that he was not siding with the Jews. Razis had a reputation as being an ardent supporter of Judaism, and was chosen as the figurehead who would exemplify Nicanor's hatred of the Jews. Five hundred men were sent to arrest him and the building in which he was sheltering was ordered to be burnt down.

When Razis found himself completely surrounded by his enemies, he wounded himself with his sword. He preferred to die bravely rather than suffer the insults unworthy of his noble origin and fall into what he conceived as the hands of sinners. But as a result of the haste, his blow failed and when he realized that the troops were coming in through the gates, he made one last, big effort and climbed to the top of the wall and then jumped onto the soldiers. They moved away and he fell down. He was not dead yet so, despite the fact that he was bleeding profusely, he stood up bravely and ran across from the troops. He stopped on a steep rock and seizing his intestines with both hands, threw them at the crowd and prayed that some day the life that was leaving him now would return.

At first unsuccessful, Razis finds a way to kill himself. We see how one man's death can be seen as a suicide protecting his honour, but one that belongs in a direct political context that can also be seen in the historical tradition of martyrdom. The death of Bobby Sands in 1981 highlights the tradition of the hunger strike and death in modern times. His death was not reported as a suicide but as political martyrdom to protest against British rule in Northern Ireland. Few comments were made about his personal mental health. Even when the coroner reported that the cause of death was 'self-imposed starvation', this was later changed to 'starvation' at the request of other dead strikers' families. These cases can be seen from a social, historical and political nexus. The then British Prime Minister, Margaret Thatcher, declared him a criminal who chose to take his own life.

In the New Testament, there is only one death that can be interpreted as suicide. In Matthew (27:5) we read: 'So Judas threw the money into the temple and left. Then he went away and hanged himself.' Previous verses describe Judas Iscariot as being seized with remorse as he has betrayed Jesus. However, in Acts (1:16–19), mention is made of Peter's speech, referring to the scripture that has to be fulfilled concerning Judas. Judas is claimed to have bought a field where he falls headlong, his body bursts open and all his intestines spill out. This is later known as the 'Field of Blood'. There are other documents that refer to Judas being stoned to death by the other disciples. The outcome is that the death of Judas Iscariot has become questioned as an insertion into the Gospels for political reasons, where Judas becomes a symbol of the Jewish state.

What this story does exemplify is the complex nature of suicide and its narrative structure. Death by suicide is open to interpretation. It occurs in a fractured social milieu where existence is being threatened. Death is in the air. A crisis situation has been building up and it is the culmination of previous acts, sometimes over decades. These acts are often interpreted as betrayal and can result in overbearing shame and remorse, or revenge and anger. Eventually, a significant person in the drama takes it upon him or herself to commit suicide. While personal acts, they also complete a social narrative. Such suicide narratives occur today and are inherent in our various cultures.

## SUICIDE IN THE ARTS

The English poet Thomas Chatterton is the subject of a painting that exemplifies a particular romantic perception of suicide. His life story, albeit curtailed, is also illustrative. At the age of 17 years, he poisoned himself with arsenic rather than die of starvation in London. He was a solitary child who largely existed in a medieval fantasy world in which his best friends were the fifteenth-century heroes and heroines that he accurately imagined, aided by diligent self-study.

Finding a store of fifteenth-century parchments amongst his father's possessions, he forged a series of poems by a fifteenth-century monk named Thomas Rowley. These were so convincing that scholars claimed their authenticity and brilliance. With such success, Chatterton continued to 'find' more Rowley poems. He also began to write his own poems, leaving home for London to make his living as a poet and writer. It was here that disaster befell him.

On leaving home, he became estranged from his family and surroundings. Although he initially secured work in London through his ability to parody the various styles of contemporary writers, this work was poorly paid. Even worse, his poetry met with no success. Failing to become recognized as a poet in his own right, his financial situation also became dire. He even refused dinner invitations from his concerned landlady and neighbours out of a self-confessed sense of pride. We see here the archetypal poet starving in his garret, suffering for his art.

Chatterton was destitute. He drank a vial of arsenic and died alone.

Here is a typical sequence of events. A boy leaves home with inflated ideas of his own importance. He loses the immediate support of his family and, out of pride, refuses any help. Such a story of a teenage suicide influenced a whole generation of English romantic poets and passed an archetype into the arts literature of the tragic young poet starving in his garret, rather than one of the narcissistic teenager overestimating his own talent and not being able to cope, cut off from his own network of emotional support.

We see the same in Goethe's *The Sorrows of Young Werther*, where a young artist kills himself because he loves a young woman who is married to another man and his love will remain unrequited. From Ovid's *Pyramus and Thisbe* to Shakespeare's *Romeo and Juliet*, we have the romantic story of forbidden lovers who kill themselves believing the other to have died. Such narratives have also entered the repertoire of narratives available to youth suicides.

In Jacques-Louis David's painting *The Death of Socrates* we see the death scene of the philosopher. He is condemned to die by drinking hemlock, although he had the choice of going into exile. Socrates chooses death and in the painting he points to the heavens, indicating his defiance of the gods and fearless in his attitude towards death. Again, we see a romantic theme of suicide from the classical literature being preserved in the field of fine-art painting and thereby continuing the idea within Western culture. The painting, from 1787, hangs today in the Metropolitan Museum of Art in New York.

## DEFINING SUICIDE

In the preceding examples from literature and the Bible, it is only the acts themselves that are described; the term 'suicide' is not used. Suicide is taken from the Latin suicidium (*sui*, 'of oneself' + *cidium*, 'a killing').

It is now believed that Sir Thomas Browne originally coined the word 'suicide' in his book *Religion of a Physician*, probably written in England in 1635. Although this may sound like a scientific work it is described more as a mystical tract and reads as the spiritual confessions of a doctor. In *Religion of a Physician* Browne criticizes some clergymen for referring to the doctrine of Stoic philosophers and, in his words, allowing a man to be his own assassin extolling the suicide of Cato. He sees this as a refusal of the Christian ideal of fearing death, which he replaces with the idea of fearing life and the belief that a true act of valour is to dare to live. The addition of intentionality, in terms of a person who kills himself deliberately, probably dates from 1728 in English usage.

Abbot Prevost used the term 'suicide' for first time in France in 1734. Prevost was later responsible for the novel *Manon Lescaut* that ends in the tragic death of two lovers. Others attribute the term to his fellow countryman Abbot Desfontaine in 1737. In Spain, the Royal Academy of the Spanish Language did not accept the term 'suicide' until 1817.

## An intentional legitimate act

At the basis of this interpretation is that the person chooses to kill himself and this act is seen as an act of self-intentionality, which is true. What is often left out from the argument is the circumstance surrounding the act and the perceived legitimacy of the act. As we have seen in previous times, literary writing sometimes sees killing oneself as a legitimate act, sometimes prescribed or expected, even though the circumstances are tragic. This questionable axis of socially ascribed legitimacy for personal behaviour is a continual thread running through accounts of suicide. We see a personal narrative of despair, whereby the acts of the individual become seen as illegitimate in the eyes of his significant others, and then he becomes seen as deviant and loses his reputation as a person of value, often becoming isolated. The resulting shame, remorse and isolation in the individual then become the grounds for the suicidal act. This ascription of illegitimacy and deviance is central to the theme of escalating distress. When people are not legitimized in what they do, feeling themselves to be deviant, they become even further removed from the communities in which they live. If this occurs within the family, then they become significantly estranged from the very resources that could help them.

If a person becomes seen as legitimately pursuing death, as in the case of assisted suicide, then this may very well succeed. What is causing concern is that such an individual perspective is undermined by reality. The survivors, family members left behind, may be traumatized despite acknowledging the wishes of the dead person.

## Suicide bombers

One particular group of suicides radically reverses this perception of suicide. Within the past 30 years, there have been increasing numbers of suicide bombers.

There is a history of political martyrdom in the Western world, using self-starvation resulting in death as a means of protest. Warrior suicides in medieval Europe and Japan were individualized actions that enhanced the prestige of the dead warrior within a death culture of honour in combat that prevented the shame of capture or defeat. Such a ritual death was seen as a rational choice, not as a desperate act, that enhanced the prestige of the clan to whom the warrior belonged and as proof of loyalty. Such acts were seen as legitimate.

As we see in Table 2.1, suicide bombers are seen within their own cultures as promoting prestige within their culture by committing a planned act that enhances the status of the family or clan. Whereas warrior cultures encouraged the individual decision of the warrior to kill himself, such decisions to die in the case of suicide bombers are made strategically by the leader of a terrorist group.

The common element in both forms of suicide is that the individual or group becomes isolated from a broader society. This social dissociation results in frustration and both an affective and moral disengagement from a broader community, which becomes the target of vengeful actions.

**Table 2.1 Contrast between individual suicides and suicide bombers**

| Individual suicide | Suicide bomber |
| --- | --- |
| Becomes isolated | Becomes a group member, albeit of a sometimes isolated group |
| Destroys self | Kills self and targets others |
| Stigmatized family | Family status enhanced |
| Mainly spontaneous or impulsive act | Planned act |
| Personal decision | Organizational leadership decision |
| Loss of prestige | Gain of prestige |
| Negative effect upon the immediate social milieu | Positive benefit for the local community |
| Survivors may be traumatized | Survivors gain enhanced prestige |
| Often a loss of belief system | Social binding to a community of believers |

In the next chapter we will see how sudden deaths are classified in modern times.

CHAPTER 3

# CLASSIFICATIONS
# OF SUICIDE

Every classification is a process in which the complexity of phenomena is reduced by arranging them into categories, according to established criteria related to given aims. Suicidal behaviour does not escape these classificatory pursuits, and thus several classifications have emerged with different degrees of acceptance among mental health professionals. We have to remember here that the act of categorizing is one that we undertake in trying to make sense of events and then suggest a response in terms of treatment or management based upon our own way of seeing the world. Different professions will have differing systems of classification. Let us have a critical look at the most common ones.

## SUICIDE OR AN ATTEMPT?

A first classification of suicidal behaviour differentiates a suicide from a suicide attempt. A Durkheimian perspective on suicide sees as all deaths resulting from a positive or negative act carried out by the victim being aware of its lethal outcome. On the other hand, a suicidal attempt is seen as behaviour that does not yield a fatal outcome and includes every self-inflicted injury carried out deliberately or carefully planned in order to obtain certain desired changes either by means of this behaviour or its present or future consequences.

This classification necessarily leads to establish a difference between two patient populations: those who commit suicide and those who attempt suicide. It is believed that the people included in the former group share some of the following characteristics:

- of the masculine sex

- in the 35–44 age group

- use lethal methods such as firearms, jumping and hanging

- suffer from psychiatric conditions such as alcoholism, substance dependency, schizophrenic disorders and depressive mood disorders.

In the case of young individuals, it may suggest the onset of schizophrenia, behavioural disorder or depression. People included in the latter group may be characterized by the following:

- of the feminine sex

- adolescents or young adults

- are calling for attention or help

- suffer from psychiatric conditions such as personality, bi-polar, substance dependence, or anxiety and situational disorders.

This classification, although very useful, should not be used dogmatically, taking into consideration that behaviours can overlap. For instance, 1 per cent of the people who attempt suicide complete suicide within the first year following the attempt, and between 10 and 20 per cent of them end their lives by suicide some time later.

The National Institute of Mental Health (NIMH) in the United States of America developed a tripartite system that classifies suicidal behaviour into suicidal ideation, suicidal attempt and suicide (see NIMH 2010). Suicidal ideation comprises suicidal thoughts and plans, suicidal impulses and the wish to die. Suicidal intention is classified as high, medium, low and null. A suicide attempt, likewise suicide, is classified according to the intentions and method.

This classification brings about a new category, that is, individuals with suicidal ideation, who admit to having suicidal ideas and representations and a wish to end their lives. They may, or may not, have a real or fantastic plan for a suicidal act. They differ from a suicide attempter in that they do not perform any act that might cause then any physical harm.

# CLASSIFICATION BASED ON METHODS USED

The classification of suicidal behaviour according to the method used is divided into *hard* or *violent* and *soft* or *non-violent* methods. With this classification there is a tendency to consider soft methods as harmless, or at least not very lethal, and hard methods as deadly. This tendency is not very objective and may lead health professionals and people not familiar with the management of suicidal individuals to underestimate suicidal attempts carried out using the so-called soft methods and overestimate the ones performed using the so-called violent methods.

Ingestion of agricultural poisonous substances is a soft method and ranks along with hanging among the most frequent of all suicides committed in developing countries. Carbon monoxide inhalation, also classed as a soft method, is a leading method among the ones used by suicidal people in developed countries. It should always be remembered that hanging, shooting oneself in the head, ingesting high doses of medication, and leaving one's car engine on in a closed garage are just four different ways of ending a life.

## Lethality

Another classification of suicidal behaviour is based on the lethality of the method, the gravity of the circumstances, and the seriousness of the intention. According to this classification the methods can be grouped into:

- *Harmless methods.* These do not imply any harm for the individual's life or health – for example, ingesting ten tablets of acetylsalicylic acid or aspirin or any other non-toxic medicine such as antibiotics, or to self-inflict superficial lacerations that do not require suture.

- *Hazardous, non-lethal methods.* These include methods that cannot cause death but may produce symptoms of intoxication and alterations of body functioning – for example, ingesting more than ten tablets of non-toxic substances; self-inflicting lacerations on the skin or in the subcutaneous cell tissue without affecting blood vessels as to require suture or body traumas or contusions; ingesting a toxic substance.

- *Hazardous, potentially lethal methods.* These are capable of causing death in aggravating circumstances as, for example, when someone cuts their veins around the wrists, involving blood vessels and surgical treatment is required; ingesting toxic substances in amounts next to the upper limits of non-lethal doses; jumping from a third floor; jumping in front of a vehicle going at low speed in a street with little traffic.

- *Lethal methods.* These are methods that necessarily lead to death unless timely and effective intervention takes place. Among them are gun shooting; the use of explosives; ingestion of a lethal dose of any medication or toxic substance (particularly pesticides); hanging; throat cutting; deep lacerations on both forearms involving blood vessels; penetrating wounds in the chest and abdomen that jeopardize the lungs, the liver and/ or the heart; jumping from a fourth or higher floor; jumping in front of a motor car going at high speed on a busy road; jumping into a pond, small lake, river or stream without knowing how to swim; setting oneself on fire.

## Significance

We have said before that any suicide method can be lethal. According to the circumstances in which suicidal acts are carried out, they can be classified as follows:

- *Not significant.* The suicidal act takes place in circumstances that cannot contribute to suicide in any way. On the contrary, they may prevent suicide from being completed – for instance, when the act is performed in public places, in front of people willing to prevent it because they have been previously warned, and in places where timely therapeutic aid is available.

- *Low significance.* The act is carried out in circumstances that are usually favourable for suicide completion, although it might be prevented. The suicidal act is performed in the absence of relatives, friends or people interested in preventing it, but in front of unknown people who can go to the spot and find the individual in a short period of time – for example, when suicidal acts are performed under the effects of alcohol in the absence of relatives but when the effects begin to be felt by the individual he goes to them immediately.

- *Highly significant.* All circumstances favour significantly the completion of suicide – for instance, when the act is carried out in a lonely place where the individual is not likely to be discovered or where communication or immediate medical care is not available.

It has been found that the above classification is not reliable since suicides have continued to be reported in patients admitted to psychiatric institutions where supposedly there are ideal conditions to prevent them. On the other hand, suicidal attempts and suicides have occurred in front of television cameras and have been witnessed by large *in situ* or remote audiences.

## INTENTION TO DIE

Taking into account the intention to die when a suicide attempt has been performed leads to the following classification:

- *Not serious suicidal attempt.* The person has absolutely no intention to commit suicide. The act is carried out as a result of a low-intensity, unforeseen impulse aimed at obtaining a gain.

- *Not very serious suicidal attempt.* There is some degree of suicidal intention and the act is performed without premeditation but with a significant affective intensity that seeks some kind of gain, not death.

- *Serious suicidal attempt.* There is a real suicidal intention but it is attenuated by the fact that although the act is premeditated, the person is more interested in escaping reality that in ending their life. He may or may not be under the effects of alcohol or any other substance at the moment of committing the self-destructive act.

- *Very serious suicidal attempt.* The person has a real suicidal intention and a premeditated desire to die. Only an unexpected or accidental event can prevent suicide from being completed.

## RANKING METHODS

The classification and assessment of suicidal behaviour according to intention to die has several inconveniences, especially for doctors, paramedics and lay people who are beginners in the field of suicide prevention. Ranking a self-destructive behaviour capable of jeopardizing to a greater or lesser extent the life of a human being as 'not serious' or 'not very serious' is, in the authors' opinion, not very responsible. On the other hand, it introduces the term 'secondary gain', a de-contextualized term to refer to suicidal people's purposes.

In this sense, it should be said that all human beings seek some kind of reward in whatever they do: social recognition and prestige, financial remuneration, flattery, or simply relief to uncomfortable feelings when a physiological need is satisfied. So every suicidal act should be taken seriously since it means that the individual has a limited repertoire for managing distress and coping with life.

A classification similar to the previous one divides suicide attempts into four grades:

- *Grade 1.* This comprises 'suicidal gestures' that cause no serious physical harm. For instance, the individual makes himself a superficial wound or mentions suicide and starts to ingest pills in front of people willing to prevent the act.

- *Grade 2.* This comprises any suicidal act that requires medical care but does not pose a serious risk for the person's life or health – for instance, lacerations on the skin that do not harm deep structures; ingesting four or five sleeping pills or any other medication.

- *Grade 3.* This comprises any suicidal act that causes mild to severe self-harm and can be potentially fatal, but clearly ambivalent, as, for example, cutting on veins and tendons and then seeking medical assistance, ingesting ten to fifteen sleeping pills and then letting other people know it when the effects are starting to be felt.

- *Grade 4.* This comprises any suicidal act in which the individual has a marked intention to end his life by highly lethal methods such as jumping off high places, ingesting deadly doses of medication in faraway places, or using a tranquillizer to avoid vomiting a highly toxic substance.

The positive thing about this classification is the way in which suicidal acts are ranked. There are no aspersions cast by classifying a suicidal attempt as 'serious' or 'not serious'. However, it provides a new element called 'suicidal gesture' that, instead of shedding light on the issue, only comes to complicate matters even more. The so-called 'suicidal gestures' are warning signs that indicate that something is not right. These signs should never be ignored because very often the gesture precedes the suicidal act.

## CLINICAL MANIFESTATION

Suicide can also be classified according to its clinical manifestation. So we have:

- *Desperate suicide.* This occurs when individuals who have little tolerance to frustration face situations with a great affective repercussion like the breaking up of a close relationship.

- *Fear suicide.* The individual tries to avoid facing a situation of which he is very afraid – for instance, the loss of virginity by a girl growing up in a strict family.

- *Revenge or blackmail suicide.* The suicidal person means to punish other people with their death – for example, when after a series of strident arguments between lovers one kills himself and blames the other.

- *Sacrifice suicide.* This occurs when death has a political or religious purpose, or is to carried out to protect comrades. The most cited example is a soldier falling on a grenade about to explode and thereby protecting his comrades.

- *Assisted suicide or euthanasia.* A person suffers and believes there to be no hope of palliation and that the situation is hopeless. He or she then chooses to be assisted in dying by another person with the requisite skills, or to be given access to the appropriate methods.

## SUICIDAL IDEATION

Suicidal behaviour has many manifestations.

A wish to die can be considered the 'doorway' to self-destructive behaviour and it represents the individual's dissatisfaction with his way of living at the moment (the 'here' and 'now'). Common expressions uttered by these individuals are: 'Life is not worth living,' 'I should die,' 'I'd rather disappear from Earth than carry on living like this,' and so forth.

We also see suicidal ideations when a person has mental images of suicide in which the individual can imagine himself hanged or visualize his funeral after committing suicide.

Suicidal ideation consists in an individual's thought of ending his own life. It can appear in different ways:

- *Suicidal ideation without a specific method.* The individual expresses his wish to die but when asked how he would do it replies: 'I do not know how yet but I know I will do it.'

- *Suicidal ideation with several non-specific methods.* The individual states his wish to die and has several options in mind but he has no preference for any one of them. For instance, he may say: 'I will kill myself no matter how: taking pills, hanging myself, jumping in front of a train.'

- *Suicidal ideation with a specific method in mind but without any plan.* In this case the individual wants to die and has already chosen a specific method but has not yet decided when or where he will do it or which precautions he will take to avoid being stopped from achieving his goal.

- *Suicidal ideation with a specific method and a well-conceived plan, often called a suicidal plan.* This is extremely serious since the patient wishes to die, has chosen a method, a place and a time, and has taken all the necessary precautions to avoid being stopped to be able to satisfy his wish to die.

## SUICIDAL THREATS

We may also see suicidal threat, where suicidal intentions are insinuated, usually in front of people who are emotionally close to the person, and would do their best to prevent it. These veiled threats should be taken as a call for help and acted upon.

Suicidal gestures also represent a suicidal act. While a suicidal threat is verbal, a suicidal gesture mimics the act and may not provoke serious lesions to the person making the gesture. Nonetheless, suicidal gestures should always be taken seriously.

A suicidal attempt, sometimes called parasuicide, intentional self-elimination or deliberate self-harm, is an act that does not result in death and by which an individual harms herself deliberately. These attempts can escalate or become chronic, and we know that the more attempts that are made, the more likely it is that the person will complete suicide.

## ACCIDENTAL SUICIDE

Accidental suicide occurs when a method is used, where the real effect is unknown to the user. It also includes cases in which likely complications are not foreseen, as happens with prison inmates who carry out self-mutilations without any intention to die, but complications derived from the act put an end to their lives (such as injecting petroleum in the abdominal wall, passing a piece of wire through the mouth down to the stomach or through the urethra).

Intentional suicide is any self-inflicted lesion carried out deliberately by an individual with the purpose of dying and that results in death.

Now that we have become familiar with different classifications of suicide, let us have a look at some myths about suicide that hinder the prevention of this avoidable cause of death.

## UNAVOIDABLE SUICIDES

The World Health Organization estimates that by the year 2020 at least 1.5 million human beings could die by suicide and for each suicide there might be between 15 and 20 suicidal attempts. It represents a suicide every 40 seconds and a suicidal attempt every 1 or 2 seconds, in spite of the fact that it is a preventable cause of death that can be avoided in most cases if direct and indirect preventive measures are taken. Nevertheless, although many people who commit suicide at present could be saved, other people will continue to die by this cause of death. We call this phenomenon 'unavoidable suicide'. Unavoidable suicide occurs in people whose impending suicidal risk cannot be diagnosed clinically. As in previous centuries, people will choose to die. The question that we must ask ourselves is, what circumstances have we created that people no longer want to live with us?

As we have seen earlier, a suicidal crisis is one in which the person is overwhelmed by his personal distress and no longer chooses to live. Indeed, he actively chooses to die.

An unavoidable suicide can occur when a person has simple auditory hallucinations that evolve into hallucinations inviting her to commit suicide. Other suicides happen as a result of sensory alterations that summon the individual to perform certain acts like: 'Jump!' If the person tries to obey the command 'Jump!' while living in a flat on the twentieth floor of a tall building, then the consequences will be fatal.

Sometimes suicide is the result of delirious ideas of immortality or omnipotence in which the individual, trusting his 'delirious logic', exposes himself to dangerous situations that may bring about his death – for instance, walking in front of a motor vehicle in motion in the belief that nothing can happen to him because he is immortal. Bipolar patients can be candidates for an unavoidable suicide when they shift from an excited mood to a depressive mood, mainly when depression acquires psychotic proportions and the individual is not in a position to protect his life.

Patients with extreme personality disorders and schizophrenic patients who are great repeaters and have used highly lethal methods in their suicidal attempts are also candidates for unavoidable suicides. In such cases the therapist should aim at keeping them alive as long as possible. Sometimes an unavoidable suicide can take place when an individual with a personality disorder, eager to achieve notoriety, commits socially reprehensible acts, such as taking the lives of several known or unknown people and after that commits suicide.

Schizophrenic patients may carry out an unavoidable suicide even during a remission period when they make a countdown of their lives and the events they have gone through due to their condition, such as several hospitalizations, or inability to found a family, to keep a job or make friends.

An unavoidable suicide can also happen when a terminally ill patient, whose quality of life is seriously jeopardized, chooses assisted suicide. For example, about 200 people commit assisted suicide each year in Zurich. This number includes many foreign visitors in what appears to be a form of terminal tourism. Assisted suicide has been legal in Switzerland since 1941 if performed by a non-physician with no vested interest in the death. Assistance to achieve death is provided in a passive way, usually by providing drugs. Any active assistance, such as helping a person to take or administer a product, is prohibited.

The group EXIT offer counselling for both patients and relatives, and support what they say is self-determination at the end of life.

Some people call assisted suicide, 'assisted dying', 'mercy killing' or 'death with dignity'. How death is interpreted depends upon the views of the people involved. As populations grow older, and the elderly either become infirm or demented, people and their families begin to question the quality of the lives that they are leading.

It was in the Netherlands that doctor-assisted suicide began in 2002. Assisted suicide had occurred before then but was unregulated. About 2000 people a year choose to die by assisted suicide in the Netherlands each year. There are rigorous safeguards, and experienced healthcare professionals must be consulted. The person must demonstrate that they are suffering unbearably and that there is no hope of recovery. In the United States, assisted suicide is practised in some individual states following the initiative of Oregon in 1998 to allow it.

Whether we agree or disagree with the legitimacy of assisted suicide, it simply reflects that the concept of taking one's own life is present in our modern societies. It is an act that is culturally available for those who determine that hope no longer exists. Where the boundary is drawn about who is legitimately hopeless and under what circumstances is a question that will continue to be debated. What concerns some of us is that in those states and countries where assisted suicide is deemed legitimate for the hopeless elderly, it may be politically expedient in times of limited finances to offer a lethal, personal solution rather than invest in improving the circumstances that promote an enhanced quality of life.

CHAPTER 4

# MYTHS
# ABOUT SUICIDE

There are various myths surrounding suicide that we would like to challenge here. The word 'myth' is being used here to denote stories rooted in people's minds that do not have any scientific basis and are often misconceived ideas about suicide, suicides and suicide attempters. Such myths need to be countered if people at risk are to be helped. Each myth tends to justify its advocates' attitudes and becomes a hindrance for the prevention of suicide.

Let us look into some of those myths and the arguments we believe should be taken into consideration from now on in helping prevent suicide.

*Myth 1: He who wants to kill himself will not say so.* This idea is wrong because it shifts attention away from people who express their suicidal ideas or threaten to commit suicide. From the scientific literature we know that nine out of ten people who committed suicide stated their purpose clearly and the tenth person had hinted his intention to end his life.

*Myth 2: He who says that he will do it will not.* This is wrong because it leads to minimizing suicidal threats as they are considered to be blackmail, manipulation or bluff. From the scientific literature we know that every suicidal person announces what is about to happen by means of words, threats or gestures.

*Myth 3: People who attempt suicide do not wish to die, they are only bluffing.* This idea is wrong because it promotes an attitude of rejection towards those who commit suicide and hinders providing help to those individuals who need it. From the scientific literature we know that although not everyone who commits suicide wishes to die, it is a mistake to think of them as bluffers. These are people who cannot find any solution to their personal despair other than ending their lives.

*Myth 4: If he had really wished to die, he would have jumped in front of a train in motion.* This idea illustrates that suicidal people can provoke an aggressive reaction in individuals not trained to work with them. From the scientific literature we know that every suicidal person faces an ambivalent situation; that is, they wish both to die and to live. The method of dying that is chosen does not reflect the user's wish to die. (Suggesting a more lethal method to the person is considered a crime – assisting the individual to commit suicide – and is prosecuted by the law in many countries.)

*Myth 5: An individual who overcomes a suicidal risk is in no danger of relapsing.* This idea is wrong because it can lead to a neglect of strict observation rules necessary with the person at risk and a weakened suicidal-risk outcome assessment. From the scientific literature we know that about half the people who go through a suicidal crisis and complete suicide do it within three months following an emotional crisis, when everybody thinks the hazard is over. It happens when people begin to get better, their movements become livelier and they are able to put into practice the suicidal ideas that are still latent in their minds but have not been carried out before because they lacked the energy and will to do so.

*Myth 6: All people who attempt suicide are at risk for the rest of their lifetimes.* This idea is wrong because it tries to overprotect the individual. In some cases, the stigma of being labelled formerly suicidal or the rejection produced by fear that the attempt be repeated is counter-productive. From the scientific literature we know that between 1 and 2 per cent of suicide attempters complete suicide within the first year following the attempt, and between 10 and 20 per cent of them complete it during the rest of their lifetimes.

*Myth 7: Everyone who commits suicide is depressed.* Suicide and depression are not synonymous. The scientific literature reminds us that although depressed people may carry out a suicidal attempt or commit suicide, not everyone who commits suicide suffers from depression; they may suffer from schizophrenia, alcoholism or substance abuse, or a mood disorder. Some may not have a mental illness but are despairing based upon their life situation, which may include their general health status, a failing relationship, isolation, threatening social deprivation or political repression. However, a current depressive disorder is found in more than half the people who die by suicide, so depression is a risk.

*Myth 8: Everyone who commits suicide is mentally ill.* This idea presents suicide and mental illness as synonymous, when they are not. However, we know from the scientific literature that in developed countries, psychiatric disorders are present in about 90 per cent of people who kill themselves. Although patients with a mental illness commit suicide more often than the rest of the population, it is not necessary for a person to suffer from a mental disorder to commit suicide. There is no doubt that every suicide is a person who suffers intolerably. We also know that some people commit suicide for political purposes, and there has been a history of martyrdom throughout the world to bring attention to a political cause. As this book is being written, there is an increasing concern about farmers' suicides in India. These can only be understood from a cultural and socio-political perspective. Notwithstanding the evident personal suffering for farmers, the root cause is seen to be indebtedness brought on by crop failures and the consequent family conflict within a cultural context where suicide is possible.

*Myth 9: Suicide can be inherited.* This idea is misleading because it leads to therapeutic nihilism. It is difficult to modify hereditary determinants. From what we know in the scientific literature there are gene clusters that may be linked to suicide. Several members of the same family may end their lives by suicide. What is inherited is a predisposition to suffer from a mental condition where suicide can be an outcome, such as in the case of affective disorders and schizophrenias. There are genetic causes for brain dysfunction and psychiatric disturbances, but a specific suicide gene has not been found. When suicide does run in families, it supports Aldridge's theory of distress management (see Figure 1.1; Appendix 1; Aldridge 1998), where suicidal behaviour is learned in a social milieu as a way of relieving distress. Such behaviours are learned as part of a repertoire of distress management. From this perspective, suicide can also be seen as recurring in mental healthcare institutions, in factories in developing countries, and as we read earlier, amongst groups of farmers. We do not need to consider these as genetic consequences but as a cultural response to underlying turmoil and distress. Indeed, the search for genetic factors masks the social factors and detracts from the real challenges that we face as communities concerned with maintaining public health.

*Myth 10: Suicide cannot be prevented because it is the result of an impulse.* This is a wrong idea that hinders suicide preventive measures. If suicide is solely the result of a sudden impulse, then it cannot be prevented. This invites therapeutic inertia. From the literature we know that prior to committing suicide, every person manifests a series of symptoms that have been defined as pre-suicidal. These symptoms consist of a constriction in feelings and thinking abilities, impulsivity, hopelessness and the presence of suicidal fantasies. If all these symptoms are spotted, suicide can be prevented. In addition, we know from Aldridge's theory of distress management that we can plot situations of escalating distress that are not being resolved and where the person is becoming ever more isolated from caring significant others and from those professional carers trying to help her (see Figure 1.1). Crises may seem to be impulsive for the outsider, but if we question carefully, those crises have fermented long before the seemingly impulsive events.

*Myth 11: Talking about suicide with people at risk may stimulate them to commit the act.* This idea is simply wrong because we know from the therapeutic literature that talking about suicide with someone at risk reduces the risk. Talking offers an opportunity to discuss his self-destructive purposes and his relational current situation.

It also offers an opportunity to talk about what conditions are necessary for going on living.

*Myth 12: Approaching a person in suicidal crisis without an adequate professional training for it, but only based on common sense, may be harmful and only delays the beginning of an appropriate crisis management.* This idea is misleading because it inhibits the participation of volunteers in suicide prevention. From what we know in both literature and practice, common sense makes us listen to the patient carefully and intently, aiming at helping the individual in crisis to find a solution other than suicide. By listening attentively, the process of prevention has already been started.

*Myth 13: Only psychiatrists can prevent suicide.* This is plainly wrong and tries to turn suicide prevention into the exclusive realm of psychiatrists. What we do know is that psychiatrists are professionals trained and experienced in suicide risk detection and management, but they are not the only ones who can prevent it. Anyone interested in helping these kinds of people can be a valuable collaborator in suicide prevention. As we see from Aldridge's model (Figure 1.1), prevention takes place when distress is relieved. Getting people involved is critical, not only because it reduces isolation, but also because people offer alternative solutions.

*Myth 14: Suicide attempters and suicides are dangerous people because, just as they try to take their lives, they may as well try to take the lives of others.* This is a false approach because it makes others afraid of facing people who are suicidal. Suicide can be seen as an act in which the individual's destructive impulses are directed towards himself. In the past, suicide was even considered as homicide of self. The theoretical bases for this idea are taken from writers in the psychoanalytic approach who believed that hostile aggressive impulses sprang from frustrated individuals. When these impulses are directed outwards, then the person is homicidal; when directed inwards, the person is suicidal. We have seen in recent years shootings in the community where frustrated school students kill people before turning their weapons upon themselves. Suicide bombers also deliberately set out to kill themselves and others, but these are special cases.

*Myth 15: The topic of suicide should be dealt with carefully to avoid the socio-political problems it may reveal.* Of course we should be sensitive to the social milieu, but where such sensitivities hinder investigation, and suicide prevention, we are simply prolonging the problem and its solutions. We know from the literature that suicide occurs in countries with different socio-economic government systems that range from very developed countries to countries with very scant resources. Suicide is the result of diverse factors: biological, psychological, social, psychiatric and political.

*Myth 16: The person who attempts suicide is a coward.* This attitude is unhelpful because it labels the person as illegitimate in their suffering and undermines preventive approaches. People who attempt suicide are not cowards but people who suffer. Labelling with a specific personality trait is unhelpful.

*Myth 17: The person who attempts suicide is a courageous person.* People who attempt suicide are neither brave nor cowardly. Bravery and cowardice are personality traits that are applied to how we regard the person committing the act and the legitimacy of the act, which speaks more about our attitudes than the person themselves. Labelling people as brave may reinforce suicidal behaviour.

*Myth 18: Only poor people commit suicide.* This is false because we cannot attribute suicide to one social class only. Poverty does play a part in despair but can be mediated by religious beliefs, strong social ties and family support systems. Poor people do commit suicide, especially at times of rapid social change, although the problems of death through communicable infectious diseases, poor nutrition and a lack of clean drinking water and sanitation are more life threatening. High unemployment rates are associated with suicide risk, but this is a complex issue and unemployment is not necessarily synonymous with poverty. It may be connected to a lack of self-worth, hopelessness and family conflict, however.

*Myth 19: Only rich people commit suicide.* This ignores the fact that suicide occurs in all social classes, and particularly amongst deprived communities undergoing social change. However, suicide is a cause of death in developed countries as well as developing countries and has multiple causes. Among those countries reporting suicide, the highest rates are found in China and former Soviet bloc states, and the lowest are found mostly in Latin America, in Muslim countries and in some Asian countries.

*Myth 20: Only elderly people commit suicide.* This idea ignores suicide as a cause of death in childhood and adolescence, and it is deaths in these age groups that are causing the most concern worldwide. Elderly people do have the highest suicide rates in most countries, although these have been falling. We know from the literature that the elderly, over 65 years of age, are a group at risk because their symptoms are overlooked or because they become isolated and reluctant to seek the help they need. Widowed men are particularly at risk. Rates of completed suicides are highest among those over 80 years of age.

*Myth 21: Children do not commit suicide.* This ignores the very real and challenging fact that suicide is a major problem for young children. After a child has learnt the concept of death he may commit suicide and, as a matter of fact, the act may take place at early ages. While suicide is the third highest cause of death for 15- to 24-year-olds, the suicide rate for children aged between 5 and 14 years is increasing.

*Myth 22: If a suicidal individual is challenged to go ahead, he will not commit suicide.* This is a false conception as challenging a person in a suicidal crisis ignores how hazardous her vulnerability is. Challenging a suicidal person to go ahead is an irresponsible act and in some countries is illegal.

*Myth 23: Once a person has become suicidal, they will always be suicidal.* This is incorrect as people are suicidal for a limited time. They may then move on from this, their circumstances may change and their distress may be resolved.

*Myth 24: Mass media cannot contribute to suicide prevention.* The mass media have an important role in prevention. Similarly, their use of stories about suicide can also lead to mimicry. The mass media are valuable aids in the prevention of suicide as long as news about this topic is focused correctly and advice is provided by suicidologists on how to broadcast ideas. Some suggestions are:

- Let the public know what the alarming signs of a suicidal crisis are. Among these signs are: inconsolable crying; a tendency to be isolated; suicidal threats; a wish to die; hopelessness; sudden changes of behaviour, affect and habits; excessive consumption of alcohol or drugs; and writing farewell notes.

- Publish which sources of mental health can be of help in case a suicidal crisis arises. The media should also inform the public which organizations and natural leaders they can go to for psychological help in a suicidal risk situation.

- Bring attention to suicidal risk groups.

- Suggest simple measures the public can use with people at risk and propose ways of asking people with suicidal risk whether they have had suicidal thoughts.

Of all the myths mentioned here, the more dangerous are the ones that deter us from talking about suicidal ideas with the person at risk, since that is the cornerstone in suicide prevention. This will be discussed in more detail in the next chapter.

## CHAPTER 5

# TALKING ABOUT SUICIDAL IDEAS

Suicidal ideas are self-destructive thoughts that can appear as:

- *A suicidal idea without an action plan.* The individual expresses a wish to die but does not know exactly how to achieve his goal. Often, when asked how he will take his life, he will answer, 'I don't know.'

- *A suicidal idea with an indefinite method.* The person says she will end her life and has several methods in mind but has not chosen one in particular yet. As a rule, when asked how she plans to end her life, she replies, 'Anyway, perhaps I'll hang myself,' 'I'll set myself on fire' or 'I'll jump in front of a train.'

- *A suicidal idea with a definite, yet unplanned, method.* The individual wishes to die and has chosen a method but has not yet decided yet when or where to do it, nor which precautions to take not to be prevented from completing suicide.

- *A definite suicidal plan.* In this case, in addition to expressing his wish to die, the individual has chosen a specific method, has thought of a specific place and has decided which precautions to take not to be prevented from completing suicide. This type of suicidal idea has to be taken very seriously.

# APPROACHING THE TOPIC

All these self-destructive ideations should be explored carefully, even if the patient does not hint at them. Communication and an open exchange about the topic does not increase the risk of committing the act; it is an excellent opportunity to start prevention.

There are different ways to approach the topic of suicidal ideation when the individual does not volunteer to do so.

## First variant

You can say to the person at risk, 'Obviously you are not feeling well. How you are thinking about solving the problem?' In this variant, an open question is asked to give the individual an opportunity to express his thoughts so that suicidal intentions can be elicited.

## Second variant

Questions can be asked about the most uncomfortable symptom, or symptoms, to discover any ideas about suicide. For instance, 'You say you have difficulty in sleeping, and I know that when it happens sometimes strange ideas strike our minds. Would you like to talk about it? What do you think of when you cannot sleep?'

## Third variant

The individual can also be approached in this way: 'I know you have not been feeling well lately. Have you had any strange thoughts?' In this case *strange thoughts* is synonymous with *suicidal ideas*. It is also possible to use expressions like *unpleasant ideas* or *recurrent thoughts*. If the answer is 'Yes,' it is important to find out what those strange thoughts are since they may be associated with fears of having a life-threatening illness, impending bad news or an imminent court appearance.

## Fourth variant

The interview can be started by asking the individual whether there has been anyone in the family who has been suicidal and, later on, asking the same question about the person herself. For example, 'I would like to know if anyone in your family has committed or attempted suicide?' (The interviewer waits for an answer.) 'Have you ever attempted suicide?' 'Are you considering suicide as a possibility at present?'

It is necessary that both the person at risk and the interviewer are familiar with a previous case of suicide committed by a family member, a friend or a neighbour. The question should be asked like this: 'Are you thinking of solving your problem by taking your life as so-and-so did?'

## Fifth variant

The individual can be asked directly whether he has thought of taking his life: 'Have you considered killing yourself as a solution to all your problems?' 'Have you ever thought of committing suicide?' 'Has the thought of ending your life ever struck your mind?'

# HINTS AND SUSPICIONS

When the individual does not 'verbalize' his suicidal ideas directly, the therapist should suspect them if the individual tries to lessen the importance of suicidal ideas by smiling or using expressions such as, 'Do not worry about me, nothing will happen.'

Paradoxically, a cessation of anguish, a feeling of innermost peace and quietness or a period of calm following an episode of agitation can be signs of serious suicidal risk, because they mean that the conflict between the wish to live and the wish to die has been solved in favour of the latter; that is, a calm before the storm.

Some other times, even if the therapist does not mention the topic of suicide during the conversation, the person identifies herself covertly or overtly with a known suicide by using expressions like: 'I am not intending to do what my cousin did; she took her own life.' Or the individual may compare her situation with a similar one faced by a friend who has committed suicide: 'So-and-so killed herself when she learned that she had cancer' when she herself is under investigation for a likely diagnosis of the same condition.

You may suspect a suicidal idea if, when asked whether he has thought of taking his life, that person engages in one of the following behaviours: speechless crying, putting his head down and staring at the floor, sudden silence, frowning, restlessness or becoming anguished.

You may suspect a suicidal plan when the person has a hidden method to commit suicide: hoards tablets; carries a toxic substance or a rope; goes to the place chosen to commit suicide, which is not visited frequently by that person; or begins frequently drinking an unusual amount of alcohol. All of these behaviours call attention from people who know the person and are part of his immediate surroundings. In this way, the person tries to find the necessary courage to carry out his intentions.

Sometimes, manifestations of anguish, fear, restlessness and anxiety express a suicidal idea that is threatening, punitive and intrusive in the individual's conscience. Such an idea may appear spontaneously in the person's mind and, although he recognizes it as an idea of his own, he has the feeling that it is an alien idea coming from the outside world that is being imposed on him. This idea, which is often recurrent, punishing and intrusive, identifies a serious risk.

As we have said, asking about the presence of suicidal ideas does not increase the risk of this kind of act and is an opportunity to start preventive actions. If a suicidal idea is spotted, it is advisable to explore more deeply the individual's thoughts by asking the following sequence of questions.

## How do you plan to do it?

This question is intended to find out the suicidal method. Any method can be lethal. Suicidal risk is greater if the suicidal means are available and there are previous cases of suicide committed by other family members using that method. The risk is even greater in the case of repeaters in search of more lethal suicidal methods. In the prevention of suicide it is vital to avoid the availability of, or access to, methods that may be used by the person to self-harm.

## When do you plan to do it?

This question does not aim to find out the exact date, but to find out if the person is making arrangements, for instance making a will, writing farewell notes, giving away valuable items, or expecting a significant event to take place, such as the break-up of an important relationship or the death of a beloved person. People with a heightened risk of committing suicide should be in the company of someone else until the risk is over, since being alone increases the likelihood of the act being accomplished.

## Where do you plan to do it?

This question may help to find out where the individual has thought of committing suicide. Suicide usually happens in places visited regularly by the suicidal person, mainly her home, her school, or her family members' or friends' homes. Other high-risk spots are remote places, places where it may be hard to find the individual, or places that have been used before by other suicides.

## Why do you want to do it?

This question is intended to find out the motive for the individual wanting to commit suicide. Among the most common motives is a failing romantic relationship, the loss of a valuable relationship, academic problems, having been scolded in a humiliating way or an immediate threat of court action. For people with a chronic health problem or a terminal illness, they may see the impending future as completely hopeless and themselves as an increasing burden on their family or caregivers. Motives should always be considered significant for the individual at risk, and they should never be appraised from the point of view of the interviewer.

## What will killing yourself achieve?

The aim of this question is to find out the meaning of the suicidal act. Wishing to die is the most dangerous motive but not the only one. There may be other meanings involved, such as drawing other people's attention to a personal plight, expressing rage, as revenge, showing the magnitude of the sufferer's problems, expressing frustration, asking for help, emphasizing a perceived wrong or achieving a political end.

A definite plan with time, date and method should ring all the alarm bells. The more planned a suicidal idea is, the greater the risk of committing suicide. The more questions the individual can answer specifically, the better shaped his suicidal plan is.

Suicide can be prevented if suicidal thoughts and their degree of planning are explored systematically, particularly in the case of adolescents who are harassed or bullied, as we will see in the next chapter.

CHAPTER 6

# SUICIDE
# RISK GROUPS

The suicide literature emphasizes identifying suicide risk factors as a valid strategy for the prevention of this cause of death. First of all, it should be pointed out that suicide risk factors are: *individual,* because what constitutes a risk factor for some people may not be for other people; *generation specific,* since risk factors in childhood may not be in adolescence, adulthood or old age; *gender specific,* for there are peculiar risk factors for women and for men; and *culturally specific,* because some risk factors in certain cultures may not exist in other cultures.

Because the characteristics of suicidal risk factors are so variable, their detection and assessment is hard for those professionals not experienced in their daily work with such people. Suicidal risk groups simply point us to the personal characteristics of those who are more prone to commit suicide, and alert us when making a diagnosis or when faced with a situation where personal distress is evident.

The main factors related to completed suicide, based on psychological autopsy studies, are: previous suicide attempts; a substance-abuse related disorder, which is primarily the abuse of alcohol; a change in marital status through separation, divorce or bereavement; a change in employment status, where a person loses their job or retires; and a major depressive or mood disorder. These are the factors. However, they usually occur in particular, personal constellations in recurring life situations.

Common suicidal risk groups are:

- the depressed elderly
- people who have made previous suicide attempts
- vulnerable people facing a crisis
- alcohol abusers
- survivors.

Now let us have a look at each of them in detail.

## THE DEPRESSED ELDERLY

Depression is a very frequent condition that affects all human beings both physically and emotionally, and has a social impact since it lessens the volition to meet the demands of everyday life. It is a widespread condition that has different manifestations. The most common signs are sadness, a low level of physical activity, lack of will, a wish to die, body pains, suicidal ideation, suicidal acts, sleeping and eating disorders, and carelessness about personal hygiene.

In the elderly, depression may present as a lack of interest in the things they used to like most, a lack of vitality and willpower, longing for the past, tiredness of life (*tedium vitae*), weight loss and sleeping disorders. The person complains of loss of memory and has a tendency to live an isolated life, perhaps sometimes spending most of the time in one room. It is often believed that this behaviour is part of normal ageing and not a treatable depression, but there are no good reasons to expect that as we get older we should lose vitality or become withdrawn and depressed. A common myth about ageing is that depression is a normal part of growing older. This erroneous belief means that depressive symptoms are often overlooked or simply not taken seriously in the elderly. Older adults can also be hesitant to seek treatment for mental health issues and often go without the help they most desperately need. Depression can also mask the early stages of dementia, so it is important to be aware and contact a heathcare professional.

It is important that friends and family members are aware of symptoms of depression in older family members. Some of the more common events and life circumstances that can leave an older adult at a higher risk of suicide include: a loss of independence and functioning in daily activities; deteriorating health or medical problems that become more problematic; the recent loss of a loved one, especially a spouse, and financial difficulties. If these situations are also accompanied by specific warning signs – like making statements about death or suicide; increased expressions of helplessness or hopelessness; increased alcohol or prescription drug use; and withdrawal from friends, family and other social support – then we know the person is at an increased risk.

Withdrawal from social contact is a cause for concern. Loneliness is the 'hidden killer' of elderly people and we know there is a link between isolation and poor health generally. Lonely older people are at increased risk of depression because they are isolated. Managing individual depression makes no sense if the person remains socially isolated. Loneliness is a public health issue too; not only does it bring emotional problems but also a lack of social interaction. It is social interaction that can mediate emotional problems, cognitive decline and reduce excessive drinking. Loneliness is a problem often overlooked and is a factor in the general problem of isolation and subsequent depression.

## Depression as abnormal ageing

In the elderly, different degrees of disorientation to time, place and person (both self and others) may be present. Older people may not recognize people, or they may confuse people and places they know; there is deterioration of their abilities and habits; incontinence may present itself; they may present gait impairments that resemble a cerebro-vascular disease; they suffer from behavioural disorders – for instance refusing to eat or be fed; and they experience mood swings. It is often believed that this clinical picture is consistent with irreversible dementia and not a treatable depression.

## Depression related to organic complaints

Old people complain of multiple physical symptoms, such as headache, backache, chest pain or pain in the legs. They may also complain of digestive problems, such as slow digestion, heartburn, a feeling of having a full stomach, even without having eaten anything. They take laxatives, antacids and other medications to get relief for their gastrointestinal disturbances, and they complain of loss of taste, loss of appetite, loss of weight and cardiovascular problems such as palpitations, chest oppression, and breathlessness. It may appear at first sight that this clinical picture corresponds to a bodily disease and not to a treatable depression. If depression is not taken into account as a likely diagnosis, in addition to wasting large amounts of resources in the exploration and treatment of a presumptive physical condition, the person may get worse and think that he has a malignant or incurable disease which, in turn, may lead him to commit suicide.

## Depression as a mental illness

The American Psychiatric Association (APA) considers that to diagnose a major depressive disorder, five or more of the following symptoms must be present during two weeks at least, and they should affect the person's normal behaviour:

- sadness and marked anguish
- a depressive mood most of the day every day
- a marked reduction of pleasure or interest in all or most of their daily activities
- loss of appetite
- loss of weight or weight gain (about 5% without dieting)
- insomnia or hypersomnia on a daily basis
- psychomotor agitation or retardation
- fatigue or lack of energy on a daily basis
- inappropriate feelings of guilt that may lead to guilt delusion

- decreased capacity to think or to concentrate, and hesitancy, most of the day
- recurrent thoughts of death or suicide
- feelings of self-reproach
- loss of self-esteem and an inferiority complex
- neglect of personal hygiene.

As we have seen, we cannot assume that symptoms in the elderly are merely the result of ageing and its accompanying ailments, dementia or a somatic condition. They may be due to a treatable depression. Therefore, if properly treated, the patient can recover their vitality and function effectively. If depression is not diagnosed and treated in good time, it can become chronic and, as distress remains unresolved, end in suicide.

## PEOPLE WHO HAVE MADE PREVIOUS SUICIDE ATTEMPTS

Between 1 and 2 per cent of suicide attempters commit suicide within the first year following a suicide attempt and between 10 and 20 per cent of them do it during their lifetime. Young men who have attempted suicide in the past are more likely to complete suicide than young women. About a third of teenage suicides have made a previous suicide attempt. Adult suicide attempters are more likely to complete suicide than young people because of the methods they use, identified psychiatric problems, and the availability of psychotropic drugs and analgesics.

While depression is a feature in people who commit suicide and attempt suicide, it does not necessarily indicate a suicide risk. People who have repeatedly attempted suicide in the past are a group at risk. Those who attempt suicide are predominantly female (it is estimated that twice as many females as males attempt suicide; see Moran *et al.* 2011), although both genders have suicidal ideas equally. Being divorced or separated adds to the risk factors but this is dependent upon the society in which the person lives and their cultural background.

Homosexual young people appear to have a higher prevalence of attempted suicide. Bullying of young people is also an exacerbating factor.

There may be an existing mental health problem or a link to substance-use disorder. The abusive use of alcohol in a family with a history of suicidal behaviour is often associated with attempted suicide and may lead to completed suicide. We know that people who commit suicide have often used alcohol or drugs prior to the act itself. Both drinking while feeling depressed and heavy episodic drinking are associated with self-reported suicide attempts. The difficulty here is that heavy drinkers do not necessarily express any suicidal ideation.

Non-suicidal self-injury is also related to the presence and number of suicide attempts, particularly in people with a history of mental illness. A history of non-suicidal self-injury is more strongly associated with a history of suicide attempts than depressive symptoms, hopelessness and personality disorder. Although injury is generally of low lethality and repetitive, it may increase the risk of suicide attempts. Such injurious behaviour that leads to suicide attempts, which themselves increase, particularly when combined with alcohol or drug abuse, are an example of the escalating spiral of distress that fails to be resolved. When this occurs in a context where employment is threatened or the person is employed and a financial crisis is evident, the risk of completed suicide is heightened. Each incident becomes an event in a repetitive cycle of escalating distress.

Suicide attempts draw attention to an underlying problem, or are a means of asking for help, and this is why offering counselling services and taking attempts seriously is emphasized. In the Aldridge model (see Figure 1.1; Appendix 1; Aldridge 1998), attempted suicide is an attempt to resolve unresolved distress, albeit dangerous and misguided. Locating the problem in the person presenting the problem often misses the systemic nature of the distress; that is, the person presents a continuing family or relational problem that cannot be resolved simply by a personalized solution.

## Individuals who have suicidal ideas or have threatened to commit suicide

Having suicidal ideas does not necessarily lead to suicidal risk. Individuals who had had suicidal ideas during their lives and never carried out a suicidal act. However, when suicidal ideas appear as a symptom of mental disorder, occur in increasing frequency, and are accompanied by detailed planning in circumstances that favour the act, the suicidal risk becomes high.

People wrongly believe that if a person with suicidal risk is asked whether he has thought of taking his life it can incite that person to commit suicide. However, we know from practice that talking about suicide with an individual at risk, instead of inciting that behaviour, reduces the risk of his committing the act, since it can be the only and last opportunity offered by that person to let us know how he feels or thinks. When an affirmative answer to that question is obtained, then we know that we have to take certain decisions, which we will come on to later.

## VULNERABLE PEOPLE FACING A CRISIS

There is a variety of factors that lead people to become vulnerable and at risk, as we will see below. Among the major factors are the presence of mental illness, a life-threatening illness and previous suicide attempts, all of which in our terminology point to a family situation of distress that threatens to escalate. Similarly, when people are forced through violence to leave their homes, a crisis occurs.

Apart from these situations, a common but often hidden cycle of desperation involves bullying and youth violence. Teenagers who have been exposed to violence or the threat of violence in a family or social situation can be emotionally vulnerable. If exposure to abuse or threats continues, the situation may result in suicide attempts, which themselves are an additional factor of vulnerability.

## Bullying

Childhood and adolescent bullying is a major public health problem in the Western world that is associated with suicidality. Cyberbullying through the Internet is an increasing public concern. The most common types of victimization reported by students are disparagement and harassment, and most cyberbullying takes the form of harassment.

Bullying behaviours are a source of depression in children and adolescents, and are also mixed in with feelings of anxiety. Both victims and perpetrators of bullying are at risk of suicidal behaviour. The consequences of such bullying also last beyond the school years. What we have to consider here is that bullying is a form of aggression that occurs in a social context of significant others, usually peers, and continues over time.

In 1999, two teenagers walked into a high school in Colorado where they shot and killed 13 people. Finally they took their own lives. Both young men had planned to take their own lives before they began their killing spree. This violent behaviour masked the underlying suicidal intentions of the perpetrators.

We can only reiterate that while factors are important in assessing vulnerability, it is the process of these factors occurring in a developing cycle of escalation that is important.

Both of the teenagers were considered to be academically gifted as children and had been bullied for years. Both young men had become isolated from the rest of their classmates. School administrators and teachers at Columbine may have condoned a climate of bullying by the athletes' groups in the school regarding these 'gifted' teenagers that allowed an atmosphere of intimidation and resentment to fester. A feature of this intimidation may have been calling the boys names and questioning their sexual identity.

One of the boys began to write in his Internet blog about his anger towards society. A friend's mother, on reading this, made complaints to the local police that he was dangerous. The website also contained violent threats directed at the students and teachers of Columbine High School with ever-increasing expressions of anger and violent intent. Both young men had been arrested for theft and were sentenced to attend classes on anger management. One of them entered into therapy with a psychologist. Both continued to feel as if they were at war with society.

Bullying can appear in different ways. The most frequent ones are making fun of other people by name-calling, disparaging comments, using obscene words and gestures or imitating physical handicaps. Verbal abuse is the most common type of abuse practised by both sexes, and the intent is to humiliate the victim. Bullying may take the form of verbal, emotional and physical abuse, and the purpose is to gain dominance through aggression over another person.

Because the target of bullying becomes marginalized or excluded from a group, bullying is an antisocial activity that requires a social context. Indeed, in some institutions, the bullying of 'outsiders' has been used to support the status quo by marginalizing seeming deviants. In the Colombine event, the two perpetrators were themselves former targets of bullying who, as academically gifted children, were victimized by the sports students. Children who are bullied may become bullies themselves.

In the past, bullying usually took place face-to-face, but with new developments in communications this phenomenon has been extended to telephone bullying and cyberbullying on the Internet. These electronic means are used to send insulting messages, as well as photographs or videos taken of the abused in positions or situations that affect self-image and self-esteem.

Bullying is a traumatic experience that harms the individual's self-esteem and self-image and may result in depression characterized by sadness, anxiety, hopelessness, hypochondriac manifestations, sleep and appetite disturbances, pessimistic thoughts and suicidal ideas. The personal isolation and continuing emotional distress increase susceptibility to psychological difficulties and mental illness with a strong link to suicide.

The endurance of chronic bullying may cause repressed aggressiveness in the targeted person, and this can be a predisposing factor for suicide. It is this repressed aggression that we see in some shootings where previous school comrades are killed and then the perpetrator kills himself or puts himself into a position to be killed.

## ALCOHOL ABUSERS

Drinkers who abuse alcohol are more likely to die by suicide than non-drinkers. Alcohol disorders amplify suicide risk, and about a third of individuals who commit suicide meet criteria for alcohol abuse or dependence. This presence of alcohol dependence occurs in all age groups and many populations. We can say that alcohol-use disorders are a strong risk factor for suicide attempts that are considered medically serious. Even if not successful the first time, there is an elevated risk of dying in subsequent attempts.

Among those with drinking problems, suicide risk increases with age. In most countries, the risk of attempted suicide is highest among adolescents and young adults but the risk of completed suicide is highest among older adults. Alcohol-dependent, middle-aged and older adults are at an even greater risk of suicide than alcohol-dependent young adults. Increased age also amplifies the association between mood disorders and suicide.

If a mood disorder is present, such as depression, the likelihood of suicide increases as the person gets older. This increased risk among older adults in Western cultures may be partly because there is an increased vulnerability of older adults to complete suicide in the context of alcohol dependence and mood disorders. If impulsivity and aggression are strongly implicated in suicidal behaviour, then these people with alcohol dependence are even more vulnerable.

A problem with alcohol dependence may go hand in hand. Alcohol abuse certainly plays a role in promoting depression, hopelessness, negative behaviour and impulsivity, and also impairs problem solving. Perhaps most importantly, it contributes a major element to the disruption of those personal relationships that contextualize problematic behaviours and emotional distress.

Alcohol dependence leads to cycles of increasing distress through tolerance and withdrawal, an increase in consumption over a longer period than is intended; unsuccessful efforts to reduce or control consumption; more time spent drinking or recovering; a subsequent withdrawal from work or social activities because of drink; and then continued drinking despite the drinker knowing the recurring physical, psychological and relational problems that occur.

We know that there is a vicious cycle where alcohol abuse affects suicidal ideation and behaviour, and suicidal ideation may affect alcohol use. The combination of depression and alcohol dependence often leads to suicidal behaviour. Anyone with a diagnosis of an alcohol-abuse disorder falls into a suicide risk group because of the likelihood of multiple suicide attempts. Drinking as a strategy to relieve distress is accompanied by attempted suicide in a dangerous combination where death is the relief. As we saw earlier, it is the survivors who then suffer.

## SURVIVORS

Survivors are those people who have very close affective bonds with a person who has died by suicide. Among them are relatives, friends, class or workmates and even the doctor, psychiatrist, or any other therapist who attended to the deceased. These people are the ones left behind and have to cope with the emotional trauma of losing someone they were close to, as friends or relatives, or were somehow connected with, as in the case of professional carers or therapists. Inevitably questions arise about the reason why the person took their own life, self-blame and how to cope with the emotional reactions following a suicide. These reactions may be physical, psychological and social. In cultures where open discussions about suicide are not allowed, it is difficult for survivors to express their emotions, which may also include negative emotions. As suicide is a significant cause of death globally, it has serious mental health implications for the general population when we consider that each death will have impacted on family members or significant others of the deceased. It is these survivors who themselves become at risk.

## SITUATIONAL FACTORS CONTRIBUTING TO RISK

Other vulnerable groups are ethnic minorities and immigrants who are not able to adapt themselves to the target country, and people who have been victims of violence and oppression. When those individuals face conflicting situations or emotionally significant problems that are beyond their capacity to solve, suicidal tendencies may emerge. A persistent feeling of hopelessness is a factor central to all of these groups.

Among situational factors are those listed below for different age groups.

## In childhood

- Witnessing distressing events (domestic violence).

- Familial change, where someone leaves or where someone new enters the family.

- The death of a beloved person who was a source of emotional support.

- Living with a mentally ill person as the only next of kin.

- Being scolded in a humiliating way.

- Being bullied.

## In adolescence

- A failing or failed romantic relationship.

- Having difficult relationships with significant others (father, mother or teacher).

- Coping with parental expectations and unrealistic demands.

- Unwanted or concealed pregnancies.

- Facing examinations.

- Having friends with suicidal behaviour or who are in favour of suicide.

- Bullying and being bullied as victim and victim/perpetrator.

- Being scolded in a humiliating way.

- Sexual abuse or harassment perpetrated by significant figures.

- The loss of significant figures as a result of marriage break-up, death or abandonment.
- Periods of adaptation to military regimes or boarding school systems.
- Awareness of serious mental disease.
- Being imprisoned or institutionalized.

## In adulthood

- Becoming unemployed (during the first year) or the realization of unemployability.
- Having a competitive wife in some cultures where machismo predominates.
- Being exposed to public shame or scandal.
- Bankruptcy.
- Recent psychiatric hospitalization.
- Hospital discharge due to serious mental disease.
- Being faced with a court appearance or sentence.
- Being imprisoned or institutionalized.
- Abusing alcohol or other substances.

## In old age

- The initial period of institutionalization.
- The first year of widowhood in men and second year in women.
- Physical and psychological abuse.
- Physical illnesses that affect sleep (chronic insomnia).
- A perceived loss of mental capacity.

- Facing a hopeless situation involving a physical illness or chronic pain.

- Abusing alcohol or other substances.

Again, it is important to emphasize that it is an escalating cycle of unresolved distress, whatever the original source, that brings about a life-threatening situation. The duration of that distress varies; what is important is that the distress has not been resolved.

**Table 6.1 Risk factors associated with suicide**

| Risk category | Risk factors |
|---|---|
| Mental health problems | Mental disorders, particularly mood disorders, schizophrenia, anxiety disorders and certain personality disorders |
| | Alcohol and other substance-use disorders |
| | Persistent feelings of hopelessness |
| | Impulsive and/or aggressive tendencies |
| | A history of trauma or abuse |
| | Previous suicide attempt |
| | Family history of suicide |
| Risk factors associated with loss | Losing a job or financial loss |
| | Relational or social loss |
| | Threatened loss of freedom |
| | Loss of independence associated with failure of physical health |
| Local environmental risk factors | Easy access to lethal means |
| | Local clusters of suicide |
| Social and cultural risk factors | A lack of social support and a sense of isolation |
| | Being stigmatized for help-seeking behaviour or expressing suicidal thoughts |
| | Healthcare delivery barriers to accessing mental healthcare and substance-abuse treatment |
| | Belief systems that reify suicide as a noble act |
| | Exposure through the media, including the Internet, to stories that dramatize suicide |

We know generally that there are some common features in suicidal behaviour revolving around mental health problems and feelings of hopelessness, imminent loss or a threatened change of circumstances (see Table 6.1). These may be exacerbated by access to means of suicide and even to the idea that suicide is a solution to resolving distress. These difficulties then occur in a milieu where the person becomes isolated or stigmatized for either expressing her thoughts or seeking help for mental health problems. In some countries there is still a stigma attached to mental health problems, and upon entering the mental world of mental health institutions, suicidal behaviour seems to become part of a behavioural repertoire. This problem of exposure to suicidal behaviour is reflected in the influence of stories in the media of suicide and websites that encourage such behaviour.

CHAPTER 7

# PROTECTIVE FACTORS IN
# SUICIDAL BEHAVIOUR

Preventing suicide involves not only public health professionals but also members of the whole community. As with risk factors, protective factors are multifactorial and involve psychological, relational, social and cultural aspects (see Table 7.1). A healthy, active lifestyle and the avoidance of substance abuse are the basis for any positive health outcomes. Personal characteristics of stoicism, humility, modesty and perseverance to achieve goals, flexibility in thinking, altruism, and sensibility for others play a significant part. Socially, we need to foster a feeling of solidarity with others; a love for the family; friendship; generosity; good manners; courtesy; respect for other people's customs and beliefs; and feelings of trust for oneself and others. The avoidance of conflict resulting in trauma and people being driven out of their homes and a healthy economic climate would all seem sensible but, sadly, are non-specific regarding suicide.

What we can see as a common factor is the reduction of distress and the concomitant development of a broader repertoire of strategies for distress management. These repertoires will be psychological, relational and social. Furthermore, because the risk factors are often culturally specific, we need to invoke preventive strategies from the milieu in which the problems occur. Preventing suicide is not simply a medical solution; it requires social and cultural understanding of the problem that engages various members of the community and specifically utilises the resources of those suffering distress and their immediate family members or significant others. Recognizing alienation is important, as this effectively removes the person from help-seeking and help-giving resources and relationships. It is also an outward sign of distress that is not being adequately expressed, resolved or mitigated.

**Table 7.1 Protective factors associated with suicide**

| Risk category | Protective factors |
|---|---|
| Mental health problems | Effective clinical care for mood disorders |
| | Effective care for alcohol and substance abuse disorders |
| | Early awareness and recognition of helplessness |
| | Early awareness and treatment of depression in general practice |
| | Careful questioning that exposes previous trauma, abuse or previous suicide attempts |
| | A non-stigmatizing approach to suicide attempters and early family or systemic interventions |
| Risk factors associated with loss | Early financial advice and counselling to avoid debt |
| | Improved relational counselling and conflict resolution, particularly when relationships are breaking up |
| | Awareness that an imminent court case, or sentencing by a court, is a critical risk time |
| | Awareness that the first weeks of incarceration or institutionalization are a period of high risk |
| | Improved palliative care and the inclusion of psychological and social approaches to chronic illness management |
| Local environmental risk factors | Restriction of access to poisons; these may include over-the-counter medications or, as in some Asian countries, pesticides |
| | Restriction of access to firearms and other lethal means |
| | Early intervention by community leaders |
| Social and cultural risk factors | Improved social and community support |
| | Accepting that we can talk openly about distress and feelings of helplessness without being stigmatized |
| | An improved tolerance and understanding of mental health issues |
| | Belief systems that support life, emphasize personal worth and service to the community |
| | A responsible media that does not use suicide simply as a dramatic device to improve viewing quotients |

# A COMPLEX SOCIAL PROBLEM

We can see the complexity of the problem that faces us when we take the example of poisoning through pesticide ingestion that accounts for about one third of suicide attempts in the world. This happens predominantly in countries with a low or moderate average income, particularly among rural populations where the livelihood of farmers is threatened and pesticides as poisons are easily accessible. In the better-off Western countries, it is medicines that are used for self-poisoning, but these are rarely as toxic as pesticides. A problem such as pesticide poisoning highlights the difficulties in suicide prevention. First, there need to be national policies regarding pesticide regulation and, consequently, coordinated monitoring programmes for each community. Then, there needs to be a medical programme for the management of such episodes if they occur. At a broader level of public health, there is a need for educational programmes at identified sites through community leaders about both safe pesticide usage and protective factors regarding suicide. Identifying key leaders to influence the community is vital, but who they are will be culture-dependent. There is also a need to identify the influential media in each country, both to improve education regarding risks and to prevent over-glamorization of the problem through inappropriate coverage. We know that there is often a cluster effect of imitation suicide in communities. None of these approaches addresses the individual and family measures for reducing distress or the macro-economic measures regarding stabilizing family incomes.

A major protective factor covers the realm of mental health provision. An improvement is supporting mental health resources in the community, and changing negative attitudes about mental health will be a protective factor. Admitting to a mental health problem, and then seeking help for that problem, can still result in the seeker being stigmatized. In a world where outward success is reified, admitting to not being able to cope is often an admission of failure. These coordinated mental health resources will require interdisciplinary cooperation and require medical, psychological and social understandings of the problem. However, improving mental health is only a small part of the overall solution.

As this book is being written, the Australian government is funding emergency measures to help combat suicide in Aboriginal communities in the remote Kimberley region. There has been a sharp increase in the number of indigenous people taking their own lives, where young people are four times more likely to commit suicide than their non-indigenous counterparts. Not only have there been a number of deaths but many more cases of self-harm. Tribal elders are concerned that the indigenous community is falling apart, which argues strongly for our multi-layered, cultural approach. Few of the people committing suicide had ever sought medical treatment for depression or confided in others. However, the influence of drugs, alcohol abuse, high unemployment and a loss of culture are thought to be contributory factors.

While emergency funding is being sought to improve psychological services for indigenous communities, as well as boosting education, such services miss the overall point that the tribal elders are pointing out – the culture is falling apart. While mental health is certainly an issue for such populations, it is important to listen to these communities rather than to apply external solutions that run the risk of trying to offer more of the same solutions that are already not working.

Another major protective factor is the promotion of psychological well-being. It is difficult to talk about this without sounding old-fashioned, as the required attributes are tolerance, resilience, fortitude, a sense of belonging and commitment to a group.

## EUTHANASIA AND ASSISTED SUICIDE

Their right to exercise freedom of choice is an argument used by people seeking to die, either through assisted suicide or through euthanasia. Indeed, the whole debate about suicide has always been about the individual's right to die and legitimizing this right. The euthanasia argument highlights this difficulty, in that its supporters say that when faced with intolerable personal suffering, people should be allowed to die at a time of their own choosing. This is part of the argument for improved palliative care – that is, the removal of pain – but there is a further dimension beyond pain that is related to the continuation of suffering. While we may be technically advanced in managing pain, the existential problem of suffering is something altogether different. And it is suffering, as a consequence of unrelieved distress and concomitant hopelessness, that is the crucial factor leading some people to consider death rather than life.

The protective factor here is engaging the person and his family in decision-making at an early stage and talking about death within a context that understands the nature of suffering. If suicide is about hopelessness, it is also about losing the purpose of life. To find that purpose now, even in an extremely curtailed future, demands that the person receives support beyond the material and the medical. How we promote hope in the face of suffering and relieve distress is a central factor in preventing suicide. Indeed, such a challenge embraces us all as teachers, counsellors, partners, friends and healers. How do we reach out to the other and encourage them to live a healthy and fulfilling life? The answer will not reside in one discipline but in the quality of personal relationships that we have one to another.

The Swiss organization EXIT emphasizes that with cultural changes in a modern world, people have the right to exercise personal freedom as an expression of personal morality in dying without suffering. Assisted suicide is seen as an act of exceptional compassion and belongs to the doctor–patient relationship when life no longer seems worth living. However, while there have been powerful logical arguments regarding the support of assisted suicide, we are now seeing more and more reports that the impact of witnessing assisted suicide for family members is traumatic. Losing a close person through assisted suicide brings about a process of complicated grief, even though the person who has died had endured intolerable suffering. Complicated grief occurs when, more than a year after a loss, there are intense, intrusive thoughts, pangs of severe emotion, distressing yearnings, feelings of being excessively alone and empty, excessive avoidance of tasks reminiscent of the deceased, unusual sleep disturbances and maladaptive levels of loss of interest in personal activities. Suicide does not resolve distress; it promotes further distress when observed.

CHAPTER 8

# FAMILY PROBLEMS

Among the main causes of suicidal attempts in children and adolescents in any social context are familial conflicts, particularly interpersonal relationships with some family members, especially the parents. These conflicts may become a suicidal risk factor in children and adolescents. The source of these conflicts may be found in problems of parental mental health, disturbances in the parent–child relationship and problems of child mental health. Familial distress may require only one member of the family to express that distress. When this continues over time, then one member of the family is seen as being 'sick' and symptomatic. However, the distress itself, while being expressed by one person, is in the family.

## PROBLEMS OF PARENTAL MENTAL HEALTH

Maternal depression is a source of suicidal risk for children and adolescents. This depression is characterized by symptoms such as sadness, pessimism, lack of will, incapacity to concentrate, staying in bed most of the day, neglect of family duties, showing little overt affection. There may also be severe communication disorders with episodes of crying spells, silence, irritability, and ensuing feelings of guilt and remorse. Children do not have the capacity to understand these symptoms and thereby become fearful and anxious. The parent may also become suicidal.

Suicidal behaviour in the child can be the result of sadness and hopelessness caused by the mother's mood, since she is the source of protection and security. If the mother's depressive crisis leads to her suicide, the child may attempt or commit suicide too.

Another suicidal risk factor is having a parent who is an alcoholic. An alcoholic father is often an absent father and creates a sense of insecurity in the child because they cannot count on their father for help and support. Alcoholism causes a chaotic emotional climate in the family in which violence, or the threat of violence, may predominate. Additionally, there can be serious economic problems.

## Alcoholism

Drinkers who abuse alcohol are more likely to die by suicide than non-drinkers. Alcohol disorders amplify suicide risk, and about a third of individuals who commit suicide meet criteria for alcohol abuse or dependence. This presence of alcohol dependence occurs in all age groups and many populations, and alcohol-use disorders are a strong risk factor for suicide attempts that are considered medically serious. Even if these attempts are not successful the first time, there is an elevated risk of dying in subsequent attempts. We also know that in indigenous populations with high unemployment, alcohol problems are central in the causal nexus of suicide and suicidal behaviour.

If a mood disorder, such as depression, is also present, the likelihood of suicide increases as the person gets older. This increased risk among older adults in Western cultures may be partly because there is an increased vulnerability of older adults to complete suicide in the context of alcohol dependence and mood disorders. If impulsivity and aggression are strongly implicated in suicidal behaviour, then people with alcohol dependence are even more vulnerable.

A problem with alcohol dependence may go hand in hand with a mood disorder. Alcohol abuse certainly plays a role in promoting depression, hopelessness, negative behaviour and impulsivity, and also impairs problem solving. Perhaps most importantly, it contributes a major element to the disruption of those personal relationships that contextualize problematic behaviours and emotional distress.

Alcohol dependence leads to cycles of increasing distress through tolerance and withdrawal, an increase in consumption over a longer period than is intended; unsuccessful efforts to reduce or control consumption; more time spent drinking or recovering; a subsequent withdrawal from work or social activities because of drink; and then continued drinking despite the individual knowing the recurring physical, psychological and relational problems that occur.

We know that there is a vicious cycle where alcohol abuse affects suicidal ideation and behaviour, and suicidal ideation then affects alcohol use. The combination of depression and alcohol dependence often leads to suicidal behaviour. As we know from indigenous populations, when a culture is deemed to be falling apart, alcohol is often the solvent that loosens social ties and is the basis for a destructive cocktail of hopelessness and isolation.

## Personality disorders

Personality disorders may become a suicidal risk factor because they are accompanied by behaviours that affect family functioning. Among these behaviours are impulsivity, selfishness, lack of remorse, incapacity to show tenderness, physical and psychological abuse and, not infrequently, sexual abuse and incest.

A personality disorder is a pattern of behaviour that differs from the expectations of the individual's culture. Beginning in adolescence or early adulthood, it can be pervasive and inevitably leads to distress. These disorders are seen as maladaptive patterns of perceiving and responding to other people and to stressful circumstances. In general, a person with a personality disorder has wide-ranging problems in social relationships and mood regulation, and these continue throughout adult life, resulting in significant distress or impairment in social functioning.

About a third of people who commit suicide are thought to have a personality disorder. Given that part of the clinical definition of a personality disorder involves exhibiting distress and difficulties in social functioning in handling that distress, then our model of escalating distress makes sense.

Antisocial personality disorders refer to those individuals who display a pervasive pattern of disregard for and violation of the rights of others and the rules of society. For people with a borderline personality disorder, the pervasive pattern of unstable and intense interpersonal relationships is the very source of their distress. Combined with swings in their emotional lives and a marked impulsivity, we see the basis for suicidal behaviour. What we need to remember is that the definition for a personality disorder contains a reference to behaviour that does not meet the expectations of the culture. While labelled as a personal difficulty, what we also have is a schism between the individual and the social milieu in which they find themselves. While undoubtedly a personal psychological difficulty, the disorder lies in a social context. Any solutions therefore need to be both psychological and social.

## DISTURBANCES IN THE PARENT–CHILD RELATIONSHIP

Most teenagers interviewed after making a suicide attempt say that they did it because they were trying to escape from a situation that seemed impossible to deal with or to get relief from really bad thoughts or feelings. They do not want to die as much as they wanted to escape from what was going on, and dying seems like a way out. The situation that provokes this need to find a way out often involves a deteriorating relationship with a parent. It can also be that the relationship between the parents is also falling apart. A way out is an *exit* – the name used for the assisted suicide organisation in Switzerland.

Some people who end their lives or attempt suicide might be trying to escape feelings of rejection, hurt or loss. Others might be angry, ashamed or guilty about something. Some people may be worried about disappointing their family. Some may feel unwanted, unloved, victimized, or that they have become a burden to others.

We know that when a marital relationship falls apart, or partners are constantly in conflict, there are consequences for the children. A suicidal act may be an attempt to keep the parents together or to mediate that conflict. When a new person, as partner to a parent, enters the family, it may also be a way of signalling that the previous distress for the child is not resolved when a parent became estranged.

Where families remain intact, the high emotional impact and frequency of conflict with the mother, a lack of maternal emotional bonding, or an excess of maternal psychological control are significantly related to adolescents' suicidal behaviours. Similarly, for adolescent suicides, the lack of emotional bonding between father and child, and frequent conflict between them, is a contributory factor. A protective factor against suicidality in families is the quality of the parent–adolescent bonding.

Similarly, parental warmth towards the child appears to be a protective factor. Impoverished parental nurturance and parental rejection have been associated with suicide attempts by early adolescents. The parents of suicidal teenagers display less warmth. A 'warm interaction' between parent and child exists where the parent is supportive, affectionate, demonstrative and interested in the child, offering time to be with the child. On the other hand, an aggressive, hostile, rejecting parent who neglects the needs of the child is seen as being contributory to that child's demise. Indeed, impulsive aggression is a key factor predisposing to suicide, and it seems to be an attribute that is passed on within families. If a family's response to distress is to become hostile and aggressive to one another, then an escalating situation will only lead to more aggression and rejection.

## Daniel – a victim of neglect

Daniel, at 12 years old, hanged himself with his school tie. Although he was intelligent, he struggled with a learning disability and was poor at expressing himself with words. He was bullied viciously at school and kicked daily, assaulted and ridiculed by his classmates. Although his teachers sometimes told the other students to stop bullying him, at times they would ignore the bullying.

He was unkempt and unwashed. Sometimes he soiled himself so that he would get sent home to avoid the bullying. To avoid this distress, he adopted a solution that would only promote further distress.

By withdrawing from the abusive school situation, he withdrew to a family where his mother was physically and emotionally absent.

At home, Daniel lived with his mother and his 17-year-old half-sister. His mother worked over 60 hours a week as a school assistant and as a part-time manager at a supermarket. He slept with a knife under his mattress. His house was described as being beyond messy, and there was debris, garbage and dirty clothes, piled throughout the house.

Before Daniel's death, there had been no intervention regarding Daniel's obvious hygiene and behavioural problems. His mother said that she was ignorant about the extreme level of Daniel's bullying but knew he did not like to attend school. His refusal to bathe was seen by her as an attempt to stay at home.

Children need support from a parent and from school. From the parent those basics include encouraging basic hygiene, and being fed and clothed adequately. In addition, children need emotional support.

A lack of parental supervision or parental rejection can have devastating effects on a child's emotional development. Daniel had neither support nor involvement from his mother. Not only did he lack a physically nurturing environment with food and clean clothes, he was also neglected emotionally through a failure to provide love and affection. The results were that he too failed to develop satisfactory relationships with other children.

## Sexual identity

For gay, lesbian and bisexual teenagers, it is familial connectedness and a caring parental relationship that are protective against suicidal ideation and suicide attempts. A 14-year-old boy, persistently taunted by his father about his identity, killed himself. Both parents emotionally abused him but it was his father's cruel words and rejection that were seen as major contributory factors to his misery.

Parental warmth within a parent–child relationship has a strong, positive impact in protecting against child emotional distress in general. Hostile parenting, continuing angry responses, combined with neglectful and rejecting parental behaviours are deleterious to child mental health. Such situations do not occur overnight. Abuse occurs over time and escalates, and with it emotional distress. Improving the parent–child relationship is one factor in preventing further distress, but parents also need the support of the community in providing what the child needs.

## CHILD MENTAL HEALTH

While the numbers of suicides involving children five to nine years old are low, the rate is much higher for 10–14-year-olds and then increases again for 15–24-year-olds, where it is the second highest cause of death. However, completed suicides are only the tip of the iceberg, as there are many more incidents of attempted suicide. Children who commit suicide have often made a previous attempt, perhaps repeatedly. This is a disturbing state of affairs because children and adolescents worldwide are finding the world that we offer them is so distressing that they want to leave it by their own hand. While the sources of that distress are varied, bullying is a big issue that leads to hopelessness. Furthermore, it is not only the child that suffers. For one child death there will be family members and friends grieving and in distress.

Children who kill themselves have often already been labelled as problematic and have demonstrated antisocial behaviour. They may have been seen as depressed and angry. If they live in a family where abuse regularly takes place, then the ground is already set for an escalation of distress. If a family member leaves, dies or the child is expelled from school, then there is an exacerbated risk of suicide. The vast majority of children and adolescents who attempt suicide have already been in contact with a mental health service and are seen as having a mental health problem. Such teenagers and children are likely to have a mood disorder and sometimes an anxiety disorder. A family history of suicide will increase their risk of killing themselves. Living in a milieu where the child's suffering is not recognized or where the child cannot express her distress exacerbates the problem. For the unhappy child, wanting to kill themselves is something that happens over time. It may be impulsive but the grounds for that unhappiness have been developing over weeks.

The reasons that children and adolescents give for their suicide attempts are that they want to die, get away from a horrible situation or escape from a horrible state of mind. Very few see a suicide attempt as a way of getting help.

It is believed by most suicidologists that children who commit suicide suffer from a diagnosable mental condition. This has been demonstrated by research carried out using psychological autopsies (Cavanagh *et al.* 2003).

## Depression

The most common symptoms observed in depressed adolescents are sadness, boredom, tedium, hostility, loss of interest in and pleasure from activities they used to like, sleep disorders, restlessness, poor concentration, irritability, dysphoria, anger, lack of energy to carry out daily activities, fatigue, tiredness, reiterative concern about music, books and games related to the topics of death and suicide, expressing a wish to die, feeling physically ill without having an organic condition, increase in the use of alcohol and drugs, loss of appetite or excessive appetite, rebellious behaviour without an apparent cause, expressing suicidal ideas or elaboration of a suicidal plan, crying without an apparent reason, social aloofness characterized by avoidance of the company of friends and relatives, pessimism, hopelessness, and feeling guilty or blameworthy.

Adolescent depressive states are likely to show more frequently as irritability rather than sadness. Changes in affect and mood swings are more frequent than in adults, who tend to have a more stable mood. Hypersomnia is more frequent than insomnia. Hypersomnia itself may be expressed as a cluster of symptoms with excessive amounts of sleepiness that also occur during the day, which then promote anxiety, irritability and restlessness.

There may be, as we have seen above, episodes of aggressive and antisocial behaviours, and these lead either to withdrawal or being ostracised. There may be a tendency to engage in risky behaviours, including substance abuse or driving recklessly.

## Substance abuse

Young adults who drink heavily have an increased risk of suicide in middle adulthood, and suicide is among the most significant causes of death in both male and female substance abusers. A strong risk factor for attempted suicide in youth is alcohol or other drug use. The frequency of suicide attempts among substance abusers is five times greater than the frequency among people who do not abuse substances. Drug abusers often have feelings of being unwell or unhappy, and although these feelings may not last long enough to qualify as clinical depression, they may increase the risk of attempting suicide.

Another strong indicator of suicide risk in substance abusers is the loss of a personal relationship, as might happen in parental separation or divorce. For young people, parental divorce, family violence, a break-up with a boyfriend or girlfriend, stress to perform and achieve, and school failure may be the triggers for suicidal events. If a young person is already experiencing an inner turmoil, feeling worthless and hopeless, responds to these feelings with anger and turns to alcohol or drugs as a means of coping, then we see that the grounds are set for suicidal behaviour. What is originally self-medication to relieve distress escalates into a pattern of substance abuse and dependence. Using a substance as a solution for coping with distress, within a relational milieu that supports the activity, can lead to an overdose by repeating more of the same solution.

## Child borderline personality disorder

Borderline pathology in children refers to a syndrome characterized by labile mood, impulsivity, poor self-image and difficulties in maintaining interpersonal relationships, which often disrupt family and school life. The symptoms of borderline patients are similar to those for which most people seek psychiatric help: depression, extreme mood swings, substance abuse, eating disorders, obsessions, phobias, feelings of emptiness and loneliness, inability to tolerate being alone, impulsivity and expressions of rage.

As in all personality problems, there is a threshold, hence borderline, where such behaviours are no longer considered to be 'normal'.

Central to this attribution of deviance from normal behaviour is the consideration that the child, or adolescent, is lacking in self-control. The emotional volatility, or emotional 'thin skin', of these children is seen as a major feature of the disorder that once led such children to be described as 'manipulative' but is now reframed as 'extremely sensitive'. Not being able to regulate emotions, particularly anger, and control expressive impulsivity leads to difficulties in personal relationships at home and at school. Family members never know what to expect from their volatile child, except they know they can expect trouble: suicide threats and attempts, self-inflicted injuries, outbursts of rage and recrimination, disrupted school careers, and a pervasive sense of being unable to help. The child is left with a feeling of worthlessness, a fragile sense of identity and a fear of abandonment. If we consider that a stable self-identity is something we manage and maintain with those we love and trust, then that necessary stability is undermined by the child's behavioural instability, although some commentators look to the family environment as the source of that instability. The use of the term 'child borderline personality disorder' may be culturally specific as some clinicians maintain that personality disorders only begin to occur in early adulthood.

We cannot escape, however, the findings that show this extreme sensitivity leading to behavioural disturbances, and labelled as borderline personality disorder, is also linked to family problems. These behavioural extremes develop within a family setting that is sometimes conflictual and occasionally abusive. Given that suicide attempts and completed suicide in children are part of a continuum of escalating distress, then we need to consider parental involvement in how distress is managed. The child with the personality disorder has developed her personality in the emotional and social milieu of her family. It may be that her behavioural problems are an expression of an underlying familial distress that is not being resolved. What is labelled as her pathology or deviance may in fact be an attempt to ameliorate a broader family anguish.

## Understanding rather than blame

We are not apportioning blame here. One of the difficulties of labelling problems is that we seek to locate the cause either in the person or the family, and this often gives the family a negative label or is seen as a personal pathology. In terms of resolving distress, blaming the person or their family is counter-productive. What we have to consider is that all people involved have been attempting to resolve their distress in the ways that they have available to them. These ways may indeed be limited through genetic inheritance, personal limitations, relational challenges, social impoverishment or cultural restrictions. Our task is to mobilize other coping resources, be they personal, relational or social.

CHAPTER 9

# THE SURVIVOR AND COMPLICATED GRIEF

The term 'survivor' refers to those who remain behind after the death of someone, or those who have survived a traumatic event. In terms of suicide, a survivor describes those persons who have an affective bond to a person who has died by their own hand, among whom are relatives and friends, and may include the physician, psychiatrist or other healthcare professional.

The reactions presented by human beings after the loss of a loved one are those of grieving. As we know, there are differing stages of grief that often include an initial denial of what has happened, sadness, anger and, later, forgiveness and acceptance. Avoidance and confrontation with family members and carers may be a part of this process.

Sudden or unexpected deaths often cause greater difficulties in the grief process than anticipated deaths. Although suicidal persons may have given hints of their existential plight or expressed a wish to put an end to their lives, the actual event is a shock, even though survivors acknowledge that they were aware of the deceased's suicidal risk.

## GUILT AND BLAME

Given that a common difficulty in the progression of escalating distress is a conflictual relational situation, sometimes leading to personal isolation, survivors often feel a sense of guilt. The survivor may feel that they have personally betrayed their own standards of caring, and this exacerbates feelings of guilt that can be destructive. The difficulty is that the surviving person may blame herself for what has happened but cannot confirm or deny this with the person who is deceased.

Some survivors may also blame other family members, friends of the deceased or carers for not having done enough or for neglect. In these cases, blaming may in itself be a coping mechanism for coming to terms with suicide and allows an expression of negative emotions. However, when blaming continues and is not resolved then this can be counter-productive for the survivors.

## ANGER AND LOSS

Some survivors may, in their grief, focus their anger on the person who has committed suicide, feeling that they have been abandoned and betrayed. A trusted relationship has been violated without any chance for that relationship to be repaired. If this occurs in a significant relationship, there is a profound feeling of rejection and abandonment, particularly if the relationship has been difficult before the suicide and there has been an angry exchange before the death. This emotional cocktail of blame, rejection and feelings of abandonment expressed as anger can be bewildering. When a loved one is lost through suicide, then a part of one's own emotional, relational life is removed. How we live with our significant others is an important part of our own identity. Feeling that we have been abandoned, and not knowing exactly why, or that maybe we could have done something to help, causes a maelstrom of emotions that are not easily reconciled.

If the blame and anger continue, then the remaining family relationships may suffer, particularly in cultures where it is difficult to talk about suicide. Having a person who has committed suicide in the family may lead to further feelings of shame and disgrace. It is then that we see the distress escalating further and another family member become suicidal. If these feelings are unresolved, then suicidal threat can last for a long time. If adolescents, in particular, become socially isolated through the suicide of another, experience feelings of continual hopelessness and have no access to support, they may themselves become suicidal.

The suicide of a significant other can lead to a cascade of negative and painful experiences for the survivor, which may become overwhelming. All who had a relationship with the deceased person will feel a loss. Once suicide occurs within a group of related people, what has been previously unthinkable becomes a possibility. As a coping mechanism, at a time of extreme distress, it becomes available as an alternative for managing escalating distress.

# GRIEF

Grief over a suicidal person has certain characteristics that differentiate it from other kinds of grief. The survivor experiences some emotions that are not often found in other causes of death. Among the most common features are intense feelings of loss accompanied by sadness, rage at feeling responsible to a certain extent for the event and feelings of withdrawal, anxiety, guilt and stigmatization. The survivor may also experience regret because he feels that he was unable to prevent the death at the last minute. Fear is present in almost every relative of a suicidal person and is related to the relative's own vulnerability to committing suicide or suffering from a mental disorder that might lead him to do so. This fear can be extended to the youngest members of the family who may be overprotected to prevent them from committing a suicidal act.

Guilt is another manifestation frequently observed in a suicidal person's relatives and is related to their incapacity to avoid the death of the loved one because they failed to make timely sense of the warning signs. It is guilt for not noticing the person's calls for attention, which often consist of threats, previous suicidal attempts or gestures, and for not having been able to achieve the necessary trust for the suicidal person to express his suicidal ideas. Some other times guilt is the result of not having taken timely measures, in spite of acknowledging manifestations of mental health impairment that could lead to a suicidal act. When guilt is unbearable, the relative can also commit suicide as a way of redeeming his or her own guilt.

In the first year of grief the individual is more vulnerable to emotional and somatic problems. Likely physical symptoms are tachycardia, arthritis, migraine, allergy, asthma and tics. Common psychopathological symptoms are feelings of loneliness, hopelessness, low self-esteem and obsessive questioning in search of the 'Why?'. This search, mainly by the parents and particularly the mother, may persist for many years.

Another manifestation of grief over suicide in the survivor is the combination of mixed feelings, such as aggression and relief. Relief is experienced as a form of personal relief after the death of a person whose problems affected him and as relief for the deceased who has ceased to suffer from his emotional problems. The end of a difficult and troubled life is perceived as a relief by many relatives of suicidal people. These manifestations that accompany grief for a suicidal person are not exclusive to biological relatives with a highly affective bond with the deceased; they can also be present in friends, workmates, schoolmates, teachers, other patients in the case of a suicide in an institution, physicians, psychotherapists, nurses, counsellors, psychiatrists, psychologists and any other person who was closely connected to the suicidal patient.

Among all these significant others, the grief reactions more widely studied by researchers are those experienced by relatives and therapists. Therapists often have feelings of personal inadequacy, grief, guilt, sadness and rage, very similar to the ones suffered by the deceased's relatives.

Among the observed reactions are wariness when dealing with new cases and exchanging opinions with other colleagues, and a variety of fears, among which is fear of the reactions of the suicidal patient's relatives: they may take reprisals, legal action or defame the professional's competence. Other common fears include their colleagues' opinions, damaging publicity and the possibly negative consequences for their professional work. Sometimes professionals avoid contact with the deceased's family and discussing the issue with other professionals, preferring to do so with only their own close family and friends. At other times an obsessive revision of the case is carried out in an attempt to find out possible flaws and manifestations that might have warned what was about to happen.

Some gender differences have been found among professionals who have gone through this kind of experience concerning grief manifestations after a suicide. Women often express their feelings of grief more strongly than men and often have a greater need to be comforted than men. Shame is felt by a third of female therapists. Male therapists do not report this feeling so often. Finally, women consider it more useful to talk about the event, while men consider continuing to work on regardless to be a source of relief.

The authors, who have also lost patients by suicide during their professional lives, consider that the reactions presented by therapists in this kind of situation will depend on several factors, among which are the type of patients, the quality and length of the therapist–patient relationship, the quality of the therapist–patient–family relationship, the patient's diagnosis, and the time elapsed between the last appointment and the occurrence of the event. Adequate and regular supervision is absolutely essential when working with people who are in distress, and even more important where suicidal behaviour is threatened or occurs.

The suicide of a child or a teenager is always a very traumatic event for the survivors, both relatives and therapists.

## COMPLICATED GRIEF

Losing a loved one is distressing. The same feelings of loss can occur when a patient dies. Following such a loss, most people experience grief. There is a period of sorrow. Sometimes we experience feelings of guilt and anger. All these feelings gradually fade. We move on with our own lives and accept our loss.

For some people, such a normal grief reaction becomes complicated. This painful and debilitating condition is known as 'complicated grief'. In complicated grief, painful emotions are so long-lasting and severe that the person has great difficulty in accepting the death and resuming their own life. In normal grief, strong feelings begin to fade. In complicated grief, feelings get worse or linger in a heightened state of intensive mourning (see Table 9.1).

**Table 9.1 Signs and symptoms that may occur in complicated grief**

| Signs | Symptoms |
|---|---|
| Focus on loss | Extreme focus on the loss and reminders of the loved one |
| | Ability to focus on little else but the loved one's death |
| | Having persistent pining or longing for the deceased person |
| Persistent negative feelings | Having thoughts of guilt or self-blame |
| | Belief that you did something wrong or could have prevented the death |
| | Irritability or agitation |
| Influence on daily living | Difficulty moving on with life |
| | Trouble carrying out normal routines |
| Changing social relationships | Withdrawing from social activities |
| | Lack of trust in others |
| Loss of meaning | Feeling as if life isn't worth living |
| | Feeling that life holds no meaning or purpose |
| | Wishing that you had died along with your loved one |
| | Suicidal thoughts |

These are, generally speaking, the main manifestations that may be present in the survivors of a suicide. Some measures to lessen the intensity and duration of these manifestations are suggested below, although some researchers have not found differences in the evolution of grief independently of the cause of death. Others, on the other hand, have found differences between suicide-related deaths, accidental deaths and natural deaths concerning survivors' grief reactions.

Death by suicide leads to greater stigmatization than other types of death and causes greater feelings of guilt, less desire to talk about it and a greater questioning in relation to what could have been done. Death by accident seems to provoke more anniversary reactions, more comments about the event, a greater incapacity in friends to understand the facts that caused the death of the victim and a diminished willingness to speak to other people.

In 2011, Olympic aerial skier Jeret 'Speedy' Peterson shot himself in a remote canyon in the United States. He had been cited for drunken driving the previous Friday and had pleaded not guilty. A suicide note was found near his car. Having won a silver medal in 2010, he had struggled within the sport to achieve his later success. An incident at the Winter Olympics in Turin in 2006 had defined his career until then, when he had been sent home early after an incident with a team colleague. He explained the reasons for his behaviour during the incident – that he was recovering from the death of a close friend who had recently shot himself in front of him. His biography included many ups and down, including problems with alcohol and depression, self-confessed suicidal thoughts, which he attributed to a childhood in which he was sexually abused, and the loss of his five-year-old sister in a road traffic incident.

## SIBLINGS AND SUICIDE

When suicide concerns one of several siblings, the surviving brothers and sisters experience changes in every, or almost every, aspect of their lives. As they have a common childhood with relatively similar experiences, one of the tasks to be carried out is to avoid their identification with the sibling who committed suicide by offering other options that do not involve self-inflicted injuries to cope with their problems. Sometimes, the surviving siblings may state that they can see the suicidal sibling at home, or that they hear him speaking or calling them.

Such manifestations should not be considered a mental health disorder. Suicidal ideas should always be explored with survivors and siblings of suicidal children and adolescents. If such ideas prove to be present in any of them, assessment of the degree of suicidal risk and psychological impairment is obligatory and measures should be taken in order to avoid a suicidal act.

If one of the parents has committed suicide, children's typical reactions may include denial of the incident, a tendency to suffer from crying and irritability spells, sudden mood changes, sleeping disorders and loss of appetite, and suicidal intentions with the meaning of reunion, although a genuine wish to die may be present. Certain perception alterations may take place, such as hearing voices inside their heads or seeing the ghost of the deceased parent. They may also start to think that they are responsible for their parent's death or they may experience some kind of aggressiveness towards the suicidal parent because of his definitive absence.

In such cases, the family should tell the children the truth about the incident, using clear, simple, accessible and comprehensible language. The children should also be provided with emotional support from a substitute such as an older family member or family friend.

Once suicide occurs in a family, it is available as a repertoire in the family's management of distress, just as it is available from some cultural repertoires. The task of therapy will be to identify that familial distress and negotiate with the survivors alternative methods of managing distress. This is even more important when another family member may abuse alcohol or medication.

A modern phenomenon related to post-traumatic stress disorder is the prevalence of suicidal behaviour among those serving in the armed forces and ex-service personnel. With conflicts worldwide in varying theatres of war, young people are being subjected to situations where violent death occurs. Although physically fit and well prepared, their subsequent mental health is challenged by events. When military personnel leave the service, they leave a social network that has previously offered them a clear and legitimate identity. If, on leaving the service, they become unemployed, which may be related to their mental health status, they lose any sense of belonging and become isolated.

## CHAPTER 10

# PSYCHOTHERAPY FOR SUICIDAL PEOPLE IN CRISIS

Before using any psychotherapeutic technique with a suicidal person in crisis, it is necessary to diagnose the crisis first. A suicidal crisis is a crisis in which, when the individual's creative, compensatory and reactive mechanisms fail, suicidal intentions emerge and the individual may tend to sort out the problem situation by means of self-aggression. Our main goals when faced with this kind of situation are to achieve an adequate time control, to be directive in counselling and to strive to keep the person alive. This crisis is similar to any other type of crisis except in one thing: the individual may try to solve the problem situation by means of self-aggression.

## SOME QUESTIONS TO CONSIDER AT TIMES OF SUICIDAL CRISIS

The stance we take in this book is that suicide is a personal crisis that occurs in a relational context. In a crisis, the first task is to reduce distress and improvise a temporary solution. This solution to immediate distress can provide a platform for further, longer-term help. Given that a suicide also provokes a crisis in those remaining, as we have seen earlier, then we can also use this approach when working with survivors in crisis who are still suffering heightened distress. Our approach has been tried in varying contexts. What is important to emphasize is that it is a network of family, friends, carers, social workers and healthcare professionals working to the same agenda. Whenever we make an intervention it is necessary to identify that network of carers and inform them about what has been decided.

Sometimes decisions must be made, and urgently. These decisions have their own consequences. When a person is suicidal and takes the decision to talk to us, there is a window in time through which we can take a steady look at what is going on and take action. This is not necessarily therapy in a classic sense, as therapy is often about change. Sometimes people are dealing with too much change in their lives. The approach here suggests looking at the situation, seeing what change is necessary and what can bring about stability, to relieve immediate distress. If change is indicated, then we set out to discover and negotiate what is the smallest achievable step to realizing that change. It is rather like when we drive our car off the road in bad weather. What we need is simply help to get some traction that will enable us to get going on our journey again. It could be that in the longer term we also need better tyres, to learn new driving skills for inclement conditions, and even a deeper understanding of meteorology. However, our immediate need is help to get back on the road. What we are suggesting here is essential first aid to get going again.

We emphasized earlier that it is important to listen carefully to what is being said and to allow the person talking to us to express their feelings. Part of that expression will probably include why they are feeling as they do. What we will need to ask is not simply the why and wherefore but also what has happened to whom and when. The following questions are a way of finding out what has happened recently and who is involved, and of exploring the problem and attempts to solve it.

## Who is involved?

While a suicidal person sits before us, we know that that person has not, in most cases, lived alone. Even though they may have become isolated, they have a family. We know that in modern times the concept of family has come to mean many things and may be composed in different ways with varying affiliations. Perhaps we can speak of a community of intimates – those people with whom we 'do' our everyday lives and with whom we are close. What we also ask about is who those individuals presented to us as significant in the life of the person are. It may be a healthcare professional or care worker. What we need to know about is who is involved in the management of distress, who helps and, maybe, who is causing problems.

## How did you get here?

How the person arrived in the current situation is important. It gives clues to who else is involved with the person. It may well be that the person feeling suicidal has been coerced into attending a hospital for help. By asking how the patient comes to see us, it is possible to see who else is intimately involved and enlist them in the process further. For example, if a husband has brought his wife into hospital for an emergency consultation, it would be necessary to see the husband and wife together.

## Who is intimately involved?

We ask who is intimately involved with the person. This is a practical means of discovering who is immediately involved in the patient's living situation. By asking who lives under the same roof as the patient, further questions can be asked about the location of other significant people, such as a spouse, partner, parents or children. For example, if asking about the location of a spouse, the answer might be, 'My partner was living with me but left after a row last night.' Or if asked about the location of a parent, the person may say, 'My father moved in next door with his girlfriend when my mother died last year.' This will raise further questions about a daughter's grief for the death of her mother, her relationship with her father, as a neighbour, and the presence of a 'girlfriend' following bereavement.

If feeling suicidal is a communication about life and death issues, it may be the management of the mother's death and the grieving process of the daughter, or father, that become the focus for the current distress.

## What happened?

It is important to ask about what life events have occurred recently. First, life events are useful indicators of family transitions, and are a guide to what an individual considers to be important in his life. These events provide a common ground for discussion as they are part of a person's life story.

By asking questions about life events, it is possible to learn how a person construes the world. If a person talks about a life history of chronic pain, where that pain continues and has become disabling and any hope of relief has foundered, then any means of distress resolution are going to revolve around an understanding of 'pain relief'. Pain, or suffering, must be addressed therapeutically. It is also an indicator that an overtly psychological approach must be made carefully.

Similarly, if recent life events about an escalating marital conflict where a partner has left the home are presented, it is necessary to address that relational problem.

## Why now?

The current situation is the focus of the consultation and it is important to ask, 'What happened?', 'Who was present?', 'What was said?' and 'Then what happened?' about the immediate past. Such questions bring valuable information about the people involved with the person in their day-to-day life and what has been happening. These questions also propose a different time frame from the immediacy of the crisis. Instead of feeling suicidal being located in the frame of a crisis, it is located in a time frame of escalating attempts to resolve a problem. While it is important to ask how people feel, it is as important to ask about what people do about those feelings. Suicidal behaviour is about feeling, but the act itself is something that is done about those feelings.

If we ask the question, 'When did all this start?', we are asking about how that person sees the problem. If we ask, 'What was it like before these things started to happen?', then we have shifted the person's thoughts to a different period of their lives. If we ask, 'Who was suffering the most before things started to go wrong for you?' then we have shifted the focus to a broader relational picture.

It is possible to ask whether the person has seen their doctor recently and what they saw her for. By asking these interactive questions, we also extend the time frame. The person is faced with the problem as it emerges from a different time perspective, not necessarily as an impulsive suicidal feeling but as a problem that has been building up over time.

## What's the problem?

A crisis temporarily crystallizes the process and focuses on the problem at hand. For a while, it is as if there is an openness of communication that allows an overt statement about the problem. Rather than seeing events totally negatively, we can see that such events are another episode where the person is trying to articulate her distress. Our skill as therapists or counsellors lies in being able to interpret that distress and promote its articulation so that we can begin to understand it together. Feeling suicidal is an articulation of distress. We need to know what the problem is that the person identifies as causing such distress.

## What solutions have you tried?

We ask what the person has tried to do about their problems. There may have been numerous previous attempts to resolve that distress. For example, 'I have been to my doctor over and over again until he could do nothing for me and then he sent me to a specialist,' or 'We tried to work it out by talking about it, but that didn't help and my friend suggested we tried marriage guidance.' By knowing what has been tried before it is possible to avoid the trap of repeating solutions that have not worked. We can of course ask why the person believes previous attempts to help did not work.

## What do you want to happen?

Once we know what the problem is, and what the person has tried to do about it, we can consider a possible direction for future change. We concentrate on small indications of expected change that will make sense to the person using her way of seeing the world. Rather than imposing changes upon an individual or family, it is the person and her family who propose what will change. A part of this process is to involve all present in negotiating that change. The emphasis here is on negotiation as opposed to one person telling another what to do, to enable the suicidal person to take responsibility for their own life. When a person sits down with us as helpers, counsellors or therapists to consider what can change, what that change will look like, when it will happen and who will be involved, then we have made a powerful intervention together. We consider that people are trying to make sense of their lives and can have the means to resolve their distress.

A warning here. If no positive change can be identified, or the person says that the change that they expect is that they will be dead, then we know that a potential suicide is imminent.

## What do the others do?

By discovering who is willing to be involved in the recovery, treatment or support of the person, it is possible to gain further information about who is involved in the family or amongst friends. For example, sending a teenager in a suicidal crisis back to a home where the father says that it would be better if his son had died is counter-therapeutic. It is necessary then to ask those living under the same roof what their responses are, or at least to discover these from the patient.

## What next?

A commitment to specific action is an important step for the individual in a crisis. As we saw earlier, the steps we take in a crisis also depend on whether or not the person can take responsibility for their own life. If there is evidence of extreme psychopathology or evident suicidal intent, then it is necessary to take formal steps to protect the patient and society. For example, a suicidal person under the influence of alcohol, who is determined to kill himself, should not be driving a car for both his own safety and that of other road users and must be prevented from doing so.

# WARNING SIGNS

There are warning signs that alert us to a worsening situation.

## More and more consultations

The presentation of symptoms to a helping agency by more than one member of a family within a short period of time is a warning sign of an impending crisis. Many of the families we have seen had been to see their general practitioner with an assortment of ailments, differing in severity, within a period of one month before the suicide attempt. Several family members may visit their general practitioner, or see different practitioners within the same practice. What links these people is an escalating distress within the family.

When people over 65 years of age make repeated visits to their physician, then suddenly break off that contact, there may be an impending crisis. There is an even stronger warning sign if they have been seeing a psychiatrist in the past year and then suddenly break off any contact.

## Escalation of symptoms

If the problem has been escalating with greater severity and frequency, of if pain has become disabling and restricts the activity of the patient, and the person become hopeless about pain relief, then a crisis is about to happen.

## She's making the most of it

If there are overt expressions of hostility and conflict made about the person by other family members, this exacerbates the situation. If the problem is about pain, for example, the family may complain that the person is not cooperating with treatment or is trying to avoid family responsibilities. The demand for a suitable 'pain-killer' in such contexts has a certain significance.

## Someone is about to leave or leaves

A threat of divorce or separation may be made between marital partners. Parents of an adolescent may threaten to throw her out of the home. Some member of a family will say that life is not worth living with those with whom they live and that the situation is hopeless. The same situation occurs in old people's homes where a resident claims that she is not understood and will find somewhere new to live, or the carers begin to claim that the resident is worse than they thought she would be when she was admitted. The social organization of a community of intimates threatens to break down, and that is distressing to those involved. It only needs one person to signal this distress.

## And it's her fault

When people have tried to solve a problem, and these attempts do not work, they become frustrated. The situation appears hopeless. They have exhausted their resources and threaten to reject the person they see as causing the problem. It is this person who becomes suicidal. None of us really likes to admit that we cannot do anything more and nothing seems to work in our lives. Such hopelessness is a factor often associated with suicide. However, it is not only the person feeling suicidal that feels hopeless, it is often the carers too. Hopelessness is a feeling. It is also a relationship.

## Change of status

There is often a precipitate change of treatment strategy whereby the treatment agency will change its treatment line from physical to psychological. This unilateral change ignores the perspective of the person and the person's family. From being legitimately 'sick' through physical causes, the person is seen as illegitimately occupying the status 'sick' and as being manipulative. This is often the case for people suffering with chronic pain that worsens. During the course of investigation the specialist decides, after exhaustive tests, that there is no physical cause for the pain and refers the person on to a psychologist or psychiatrist. It is then that an overdose of pain tablets is taken. When this happens the family believes they have been tricked and their worst suspicions are confirmed. The family look over past events and the person is then seen as having been illegitimate in their claims to be physically sick. A pain patient moves from the status of being legitimate in their claim to being sick, to the stigmatized status of a psychiatric case.

## No matter what you do, it is wrong

Finally, any attempts to resolve distress, or any actions by the persons involved, are seen as further acts of willed defiance or being uncooperative. The individual sees anything the family tries to do as a rejection, or the individual feels that the family rejects what she tries to do. Both sides say 'no' to the existence of the other. This mutual rejection can just as well apply in healthcare organisations, social institutions, educational establishments and care agencies, as well as in families.

Sometimes, diagnosing a suicidal crisis is easy because the individual expresses his wish to end his life by suicide. At other times it is necessary to explore whether suicidal ideas exist. We have mentioned some ways of doing it, although for many therapists the best way to detect suicidal risk is by asking the person if he or she has had suicidal ideas. Of course, a suicidal crisis differs when it appears in a child, an adolescent, an adult or an elderly person, so it is necessary to become familiar with some of the principal characteristics of suicidal behaviour in each of these stages of life because the treatment will also differ.

# SOME CONSIDERATIONS FOR COUNSELLING

Unbearable psychological suffering can be reduced by listening intently to what the other is saying, and then allowing them free emotional expression. Psychological needs should be acknowledged as real. The principal emotion of suicide is hopelessness. Death is sometimes considered as an escape from this suffering and hopelessness. Therefore, we need to find alternative solutions to resolve current distress, emphasizing that death by suicide is a permanent and irrevocable solution. We can, however, find temporary solutions that may bring some relief, which themselves offer a glimmer of hope.

The main aim of suicide for the individual is often the cessation of consciousness rather than death; that is, to stop thinking and feeling. This aim may indicate the need for immediate medication. However, some people may have already used alcohol or self-medicated to achieve relief through unconsciousness, and medication may simply repeat an already failed solution.

Ambivalence is present in all suicides and these individuals wish both to die and to continue to live at the same time, so it is necessary to detect this attitude and help the individual decide to choose to live. Talking about death directly can also prompt talking about living. It is important for the counsellor or therapist herself not to become 'anxious' when talking about death, as this undercurrent of anxiety may be transferred back to the other person.

Some people may try to send messages about their suicidal intentions but these are often indirect. It is important for the therapist to ask about suicidal ideas or intentions directly.

If aggression is present, or the person is known to be impulsive, then the risk is heightened.

There may have been suicidal behaviour in the person's past, so it is important to make a life history review and discover how the person has coped with such feelings or situations previously in managing distress.

We emphasize strongly the importance of supervision for the counsellor or therapist who has contact with people who have become suicidal and despairing. Despair can be contagious.

## Psychological first aid

Psychological first aid can be offered by anyone provided that the recommendations described in Table 10.1 are followed at each stage. Table 10.1 summarizes the technique by emphasizing what the therapist, counsellor or carer should and should not do when dealing with an individual in suicidal crisis.

**Table 10.1 Stages of psychological first aid**

| Stage | Do | Do not |
|---|---|---|
| I. Establish contact | Listen. | Tell your own story. |
| | Show feelings. | Ignore feelings. |
| | Accept that the problem the person says is important is important. Speak clearly (the person may be hard of hearing). | Minimize the importance of psychological needs or problems. |
| II. Learn the dimension of the problem | Frame open questions to ease communication about feelings. | Ask Yes/No questions. |
| | Assess suicidal risk. Ask straightforwardly if necessary about intentions and plans, about how and when and with what means they intend to take their own life. | Ignore or neglect suicidal risk. |
| | Talk about death and dying and what that means for the person. | Avoid talking about death. |
| III. Possible solutions | Ask about what has been tried to solve the problem before. | Ignore previous attempted solutions. |
| | Establish priorities to relieve distress. | Approach the problem with tunnel vision. |
| IV. Concrete action | Take timely measures. | Hesitate. |
| | Be directive; confront if necessary. | Neglect responsibilities. |
| V. Follow-up | Re-evaluate outcome of session yourself. | Refer the patient after outcome self-evaluation to another therapist. |

An important aspect in a potential suicide's psychotherapy is to provide information about the location of local mental health institutions that can provide help during crisis situations, the location of such places and how to get to them, when to go to them for help, what kind of help they offer, and what their opening hours are. If there are emergency counselling services, social work or mental health interventions, then write down a telephone number.

Although people become desperate and their suicidal fantasies become stronger, this may be because they are alone with those fantasies. Once they come into contact with another person who listens, they may be amenable to help.

If an individual confesses a wish to die, the following suggestions may be of help:

- Do not become alarmed; just take that person seriously.

- Encourage him to speak about his problems and how he feels about them.

- Ask about how he has tried to solve his problems in the past and what has been effective, or not!

- Allow the person to talk about his suffering.

- In some cultures, it may be comforting to provide physical contact by holding a person's hand or a light touch on the forearm.

- Do not use yourself as an example. Do not talk about yourself or your personal experiences.

- Do not suggest solutions that worked for you in the past. Such solutions may not work for the patient.

- Ask what the smallest possible step would be to achieve a change for the better.

- If you are not sure about what you are doing, ask for help. It is not advisable to manage suicidal people alone when you feel insecure.

- Stay with that person until the crisis is over. You will know it when the person is able to reflect critically and verbally about suicidal thoughts, his mood has improved, and he becomes more relaxed, calm, cooperative and interested in daily routines.

- If the suicidal risk persists, make arrangements for the individual to receive specialized psychiatric treatment.

- Talking to an individual in suicidal crisis about the positives you may see in his life is not recommended since that is precisely what he is not able to see.

- Avoid any feelings in yourself about being manipulated or that the person is attention-seeking. These feelings are easily transferred to the other person and are unhelpful in the situation. These feelings can be brought up later in supervision. The person is indeed trying to bring about change, and maybe to your way of thinking, illegitimately but the first task is to remove the immediate distress.

## SUICIDAL CRISIS IN CHILDHOOD

It is believed that children under five or six years of age have a very elementary idea of what death and dying mean. At this age, death is represented, personified or objectified as either a good-meaning or bad-meaning person or as a pleasant or an unpleasant place. Children commonly associate death with old age or disease. Over this age, death begins to be viewed as an unavoidable or universal event and the child may come to the conclusion that all people, including themselves, have to die.

Children may have had some experience of the topic since they may have seen soaps and other dramas that portray situations in which a character has taken their life on television. Sometimes the concept is grasped through dialogues with other children of their age who have had suicidal relatives or have heard adult conversations.

A child's concept of suicide is a blend of rational and irrational, articulated and logical and not very coherent and understandable beliefs. Some children grasp the concepts of death and suicide at an earlier age than others. Before acquiring these concepts, children believe that death is a continuum of life, a state resembling sleep from which a person can be awakened, as in the story 'Sleeping Beauty'.

During a suicidal crisis children experience a number of behavioural signs that consist of all sorts of changes. They may become aggressive or passive in school or at home. Their eating and sleeping habits also change; they may become anorexic and refuse food or, on the contrary, exhibit an unusually voracious appetite. Concerning their sleeping habits, the changes may appear as sleeplessness, night panic, nightmares, bed-wetting or excessive sleepiness.

Similarly, a suicidal crisis may also be seen in poor school achievement, running away from school, lack of interest in studying, and rebelliousness without an apparent cause. The child no longer takes part in games with friends, may give away their belongings and write farewell notes. Such a crisis is situated in a family environment or caring environment. For that reason, it is essential to provide therapeutic treatment involving the parents or carers. For children in a residential setting, it is vital to include the people involved in their everyday care.

Psychotherapy for a child needs to be aimed at promoting an understanding by parents, teachers or carers that changing events in the child's environment may presage the occurrence of a suicidal act, and at identifying what distress is trying to be resolved. It is important to emphasize here the need to have control over the methods the child might use to harm herself and to recognize any possible precipitating factors, like the fear of being punished or being humiliated, known problems at school, or having witnessed painful events.

We try to avoid by all means the parents blaming each other. Instead, we try to help them see that we already have a problem in the family, the child's self-destructive behaviour, so we do not need to add a new problem. What we can do is to see what the parents or carers have already tried to do to solve the problem. If that has not worked then we can avoid repeating it. However, we can negotiate new solutions with the family and the child to resolve the problem.

This involves the expertise of the therapist and the family, including the child. The family may be extended to include wider family members if they are available. In situations where family members are not available, then we bring together those people in the immediate milieu of the child.

Family members should never feel that this type of behaviour is intended to manipulate them; on the contrary, they are encouraged to see that they have the resources to resolve daily problems. Family management includes not only the treatment of the child's suicidal crisis, but also the aim of achieving an adequate family functioning that prevents further suicidal acts by negotiating other forms of distress management.

## Hospitalization

Hospitalization of the child is recommended if a suicidal attempt has been carried out using a highly lethal method; that is, if the intention was to die, if suicidal planning persists or if the suicidal attempt is the onset of a psychiatric disease with serious psychotic symptoms. The same applies if the attempt is associated with addictive substance abuse or where abuse is present, if the parents suffer from any psychiatric disorder, and if the family cannot take responsibility for the child's outpatient treatment.

# SUICIDAL CRISIS IN ADOLESCENCE

Generally speaking, suicidal behaviour in adolescence can be divided into three stages:

1. A problematic childhood characterized by a number of events, which may include paternal abandonment, a broken home, the death of loved ones by suicide, paternal alcoholism, maternal depression, socio-economic difficulties, and sexual, physical or psychological abuse.

2. Recurrence of the previous problems plus those typical of adolescence, relating to sexual identity, bodily changes, new challenges in social relationships, unshared parental expectations, an unsupported wish for independence and the challenge of making vocational choices.

3. A pre-suicidal stage characterized by the rupture of a valuable relationship, a challenging situation with authority (like appearing in court or before a school disciplinary committee) or an unexpected change in the adolescent's daily routine, which he cannot manage in a creative and satisfactory way.

It means that when you are in front of a potentially suicidal adolescent it is paramount to look into his biography to pinpoint possible critical events that might be potential risk factors and to see how he has adapted to adversity in the past.

It is more difficult to detect a suicidal crisis in adolescence than in childhood, in spite of the frequency with which these acts appear in adolescence. While suicidal attempts can occur at any age, completed suicide is the second or third cause of death in the 15–19 age group in many countries. If we take this reality into consideration, recognizing the signs that define a suicidal crisis in adolescence is a priority. In so doing it is necessary to keep in mind the following familial and personal indicators.

## Familial situation

The likelihood of suicidal adolescents coming from a dysfunctional family is higher than from non-suicidal adolescents; suicidal adolescents have more difficulties in their relationships with their parents and lack the necessary emotional and psychological support to face vital events; they come from broken homes as a result of divorce, separation or death of one of the parents, sometimes by suicide.

## Personal situation

Suicidal adolescents have several symptoms that can be caused by an underlying mental disease. A depressive disorder is one of the most frequent ones. Significant changes in emotion are very common and they are characterized by a lack of interest in daily affairs, aggressiveness, rebelliousness, disobedience, withdrawal, sleeping and feeding disorders, health concerns, death thoughts and suicidal ideas with some degree of planning. Some adolescents do not feel pleasure any more in doing the activities they used to like doing. Their capacity to concentrate becomes smaller. Once-pleasant experiences are no longer perceived as such, and feelings of loneliness, hopelessness, helplessness, guilt and uselessness appear.

We often see the onset of schizophrenia occurring in adolescence, and suicidal behaviour may be the first of the symptoms to appear. Schizophrenia is suspected if a strange behaviour appears that does not fit the adolescent's past history.

Some adolescents do not suffer from a psychiatric disease but have other signs that must be identified in order to prevent a suicidal act. The most common ones are impulsivity, planning difficulties, cognitive rigidity and an inflexibility in finding new solutions to problems. This inflexibility is what we refer to as a limited repertoire of strategies for managing distress. If every time an adolescent has a problem, or even thinks they may have an impending problem, they misuse medication, begin drinking, have a violent outburst or run away, then we can say that they have a limited repertoire for managing distress. These are all available responses within our Western cultures and part of the narratives we see in modern entertainment media. However, in the everyday life of the adolescent and his family they can be destructive.

Prior to committing a suicidal act, an adolescent's behaviour may be characterized by an excessive consumption of alcohol or abuse of drugs. Precursors often include the loss of a valuable relationship, suicidal threats, social detachment, expressions of anguish, crying spells, writing farewell notes to friends, increasing loneliness, an inability to cope with a painful situation, a negative perception of self and negativity about the present and a loss of hope for the future.

## DEALING WITH A SUICIDAL CRISIS

When facing a suicidal crisis in adolescents, we should keep in mind the following principles:

- Treat the person with respect.

- Take the person seriously.

- Believe what is being said.

- Listen intently.

- Let the person express painful emotions.

- Explore the presence of suicidal ideas.

- Work together to find non-suicidal solutions.

- If possible, establish a no-suicide contract.

- Request consent to involve relatives and friends who can be of help.

- Establish clear guidelines about who is to be contacted during a suicidal crisis.

- If psychopharmacological treatment is necessary, establish that the person understands the dosage and is compliant about using medication.

- Do not judge. Promise not to reveal the patient's confessions about suicidality. (However, this confidentiality may have to be revised in the case of child abuse or the perpetration of child abuse by the patient.)

It is also important to find out about any close friends who can be involved in the suicidal crisis therapy. Communication with peers is extremely important provided that the situation and the main goal – preventing the patient from harming himself – are explained clearly.

The family need to be informed that a suicidal act should be taken seriously, that it is not a bluff, a show or mere manipulation, and that it means that something is wrong in the adolescent's world. The family can be invited to make an inventory or keep a diary of the events and situations that might be responsible for such behaviour and invited to offer possible means of resolving problems and distress. A first step is to identify the problem that is causing distress and propose a way of relieving that distress, even if only temporarily, to gain a period of relief to instigate further therapeutic interventions.

How often the adolescent is seen by the therapist depends upon the presence of suicidal ideas and, if any exist, the extent of planning. It is also absolutely vital to recognize the presence of any depressive symptoms being presented by the person and requiring the presence of a trained mental health professional.

In an adolescent who has attempted suicide or exhibited suicidal behaviour, it is advisable to discuss the consequences the suicidal act might bring about for her life and her relationship with other people, and the consequences of her dying for family and friends. It may be that the she has already thought this through and is planning an act of attrition, but more often than not, at times of heightened and unbearable personal distress, thoughts of loved ones are forgotten. Discussing considerations about others is not aimed at promoting guilt but at emphasizing another point of view and eliciting responses from family members and friends. If a young person has thought about the consequences and still has a plan of action, that person is likely to go ahead with suicidal acts.

Friends and acquaintances can have opinions and points of view about those who are suicidal that may range from compassion to total rejection. A person who makes attempts against his life provokes strong emotions in those people who also take part in his daily life. These emotions may be negative. By taking a problem-solving strategy involving family, friends or carers it is possible to switch from an overloaded emotional situation to one that is based on practical actions. This is not to deny that there is obviously an emotional content to suicidal behaviour and that emotions belong to relationships, some of which may already be conflictual.

Particularly with adolescents, it is necessary to remove the emotional heat from the situation while recognizing the distress, and to take a pragmatic step in resolving that distress with all involved.

If the parents feel too guilty about what has happened, it is necessary to lessen their culpability to prevent them from committing new mistakes with the adolescent and, instead of trying to ease the situation, may make it even worse. We can remind the parents that since their child was born, they have surely done everything they could to keep him safe. In other words, we try to make the parents aware of the fact that when their child's life depended completely or to a great extent on them, they did what was expected of them. Now it is the adolescent who has to make personal decisions and life choices. This kind of therapy has been used successfully with adolescents where there is not an overwhelming presence of mental illness and where they live in a family environment with no significant disintegration.

Some people harm themselves to avoid physical pain. The symptom need not be present; the patient may want to take his life just to avoid what is in store for him, as in the case of incurable diseases. In a situation like this, it is advisable to guarantee the patient that medication is available in sufficient amounts to face his condition and that, if it fails, there are alternative techniques as part of palliative care to fight the pain. In these situations, particularly where pain medication is not working, it is essential that therapists and clinicians understand the difference between pain and suffering. If the distress of pain is not being reduced with medication, then we must be alerted to the presence of the distress that suffering causes. Here again, we emphasize that in terms of distress management, and particularly in the case of suffering, medication may be a restricted strategy in a limited repertoire.

Some people resort to suicidal behaviour as a way of asking for help or to sort out problems they are not capable of facing by themselves. It is possible to remove the person from the situation as a temporary respite. However, the long-term aim of therapy is to find solutions that are appropriate and available to the young person. We are using the word 'available' in the sense that they exist within her social milieu and are also psychologically and emotionally possible.

When an adolescent wishes to die, reflecting with them about the supposed goodness and advantages of being alive is not recommended, because that is precisely what the adolescent is not able to see at the time. However, it may be possible to negotiate a postponement of suicidal behaviour by means of a 'no-suicide contract'. Of course, this only works if the person agrees not to violate it, but a realistic agreement is part of the negotiation. There are no guarantees, so such an agreement needs careful assessment. No-suicide contracts should not be used with adolescents who are mentally disturbed and do not have the necessary family or social support and adequate contact.

While we wait for the suicidal crisis to be over, we try to take advantage of time to find non-destructive ways out of a distressing situation. Sometimes adolescents accept hospitalization as long as everybody benefits from the measures proposed, especially the adolescent. In that case, the adolescent should be admitted for a short period of time until he is capable of protecting himself from his destructive impulse.

A commonsense approach suggests exploring the existence of suicidal ideas, listening carefully and finding non-suicidal solutions. If the exploration of suicidal ideas reveals that the adolescent has made previous attempts, has a detailed suicidal plan, and has considered what will happen after death and the disposal of his possessions, then residential psychiatric care is called for.

## SUICIDAL CRISIS IN THE ADULT

It is easier to detect signs of suicidal crisis in adults than in children and adolescents. As a rule, adults are better at communicating their suicidal thoughts than younger people. Adults may communicate their suicidal thoughts either verbally or non-verbally by means of gestures and threats. When an adult admits to having suicidal intentions, the first thing a therapist should do is to evaluate whether the individual is able to take responsibility for his own life. It is important to determine the presence of previous suicide attempts and the methods used in those attempts, which psychiatric or somatic conditions this person has suffered from, whether he has had previous psychiatric hospitalizations, any previous or current mental health treatment, current life changes and the extent, or lack, of family or social contacts.

It is important to seek the healthy parts of the individual's personality, as well as finding the resources she has to face life and evaluating mental health status. One avenue to explore is the reasons the individual has to go on living. Here the therapist should evaluate the quality of the individual's marital relationship, her job satisfaction, the quality of the relationship with her children if she has any, her physical and mental health status, and her social adaptability, which comprises her sense of belonging to groups with similar ambitions, moral principles and convictions.

## Personal responsibility (the Pérez Barrero approach)

While we may argue that as adults we are all responsible for our own lives, this belies the reality of everyday living and also cuts us off from our social responsibilities to each other. There is a spectrum of personal responsibility, but we will suggest three categories here simply as a rule of thumb.

1. *A limited capacity for taking responsibility.* In this category we find people who have few reasons to continue living. They may be lonely elderly people who have no relatives to take care of them, who have become isolated and have a painful chronic illness. This is exacerbated by poverty, alcohol abuse and insomnia. We may also include here individuals with severe psychiatric conditions such as schizophrenia, depression and complicated alcoholism.

2. *People who retain some responsibility.* This category includes people affected by the conditions mentioned in the previous category yet manage to maintain contact with a healthcare professional or social worker, can be managed at home and do not have severe symptoms. In this category are also people with mental health problems but who have access to and utilize regularly a social network. Such a social network may be social workers or care workers, but there is regular social contact.

3. *People with full responsibility for their lives*. Even though they may have mental health problems, or be facing emotional challenges or have a physical disease, they can manage their own lives. They have active contacts with family or friends where they can express themselves, including their feelings.

Each of these categories needs a different kind of intervention technique, as shown in Table 10.2.

We would like to emphasize that there is no sense in being dogmatic about intervention techniques. However, if the situation is of high risk the therapist must become active and take steps to protect the person.

Suicide attempters and people who become suicidal are often desperate, confused and vulnerable, and may have an ambivalent blend of feelings. What has usually happened is that they have run out of resources for relieving distress. When faced with this type of situation, it is advisable to provide a structured relationship, offering frequent emotional support and help in problem solving. This will include helping them consider their relational difficulties and will involve other people such as family members, fellow workers or school friends to lessen the feelings of loneliness and helplessness, which so often emerge in suicidal people. It will also involve resolving conflict.

It is good to know how the individual feels about his life and why he thinks he must end it by suicide, since discussing those issues may bring about relief. It should always be kept in mind that people may see themselves as having a very narrow range of alternatives to choose from, which reduces itself to only one: suicide. Therefore, it is very important to listen carefully to see how realistic are the solutions they have in mind for their problems and to explore the existence of suicidal ideas. Talking about death can be encouraged. Not everybody who embarks upon suicidal behaviour wishes to die, but most find it difficult to talk about living. Paradoxically, talking about dying and its consequences can highlight what a person considers important about continuing to live and what must change in their circumstances to go on living.

**Table 10.2 Differing therapeutic relationships according to perceived personal responsibility in the Pérez Barrero approach**

| Category | Intervention technique |
| --- | --- |
| Individuals who have only a limited capacity for taking responsibility of their lives | An active, directive therapeutic relationship is indicated. Suicidal behaviour should be considered a possibility, given the person's state of mind. If the person is aggressive, impulsive, and has become isolated, then risk is enhanced. |
| | Underlying health problems need to be treated urgently, particularly if they are associated with pain and suffering and/or alcohol/substance abuse. It may be necessary to institutionalize the person under a mental health order. |
| | We must bear in mind that hospitalization, or release from a psychiatric hospital stay, is also a risk factor. |
| | The familial situation or social setting needs to be assessed to see which factors may be exacerbating the problem and if there is any imminent change. |
| | It is important to ask questions about potential legal proceedings that the person sees as a threat against himself. |
| | Once a crisis has been averted, it is necessary to negotiate another form of therapeutic relationship. |
| People who have retained some responsibility for their lives | A cooperative, but guided, therapeutic relationship is to be encouraged. |
| | Again, this relationship will depend upon the familial or social support available. Help by the individual's family and friends can be requested to help reduce distress. |
| | If appropriate ways of reducing personal, relational or familial distress can be found, and there is no immediate threat or suicide plan, then structured, supervised counselling is appropriate. |
| | It is important to assess what threats there are to the person regarding self-aggression or from others. If the person is being bullied, a systemic approach must be undertaken. |
| | Note that substance or alcohol abuse complicates the therapeutic situation. |

| Individuals fully responsible for their lives | Despite suicidal thoughts or a suicide attempt, the situation requires a therapeutic relationship based on mutual participation. |
| --- | --- |
| | It is important to discuss the immediate distress and take steps to remove that. |
| | It is important to establish that the person feels that they have responsibility for their own life and the impact the suicidal behaviour has on their immediate surroundings. |
| | Life goals and personal fulfilment, including personal relationships, can be explored. |
| | Family and social support can be recruited if appropriate. |

# SUICIDAL CRISIS IN THE ELDERLY

An older person is less likely to make a suicide attempt and more likely to complete suicide and use a highly lethal method such as a firearm, hanging or overdosing with medication or other forms of drugs. Suicide occurs at a high rate in elderly people in most countries and is linked to a psychiatric disorder, predominantly depression and high levels of hopelessness. Alcohol abuse may also be a contributory factor, particularly when an older person has fewer cognitive resources to cope with the adaptive challenges of ageing. As we have seen earlier, alcohol is a dangerous coping solution.

Fewer warning signs are apparent, although the act itself is premeditated and has its own logic. One particular concern is that people over 60 years have often had increased contact with general practitioners and physicians in the year before the suicide (Deisenhammer et al. 2007). While this 'doctor shopping' may be an indication of searching for help, it may just as well reflect a strategy for collecting a lethal medication cocktail. Although contact with a physician occurs more frequently in the year before the incident, shortly before that incident, contact with the physician or psychiatrist is broken off. In addition, suicide intent is then rarely communicated during the consultations prior to the incident. This pattern of intense contact with the physician and then a sudden disruption of the therapeutic relationship, in that the patient does not show up any more, is a cause for concern and counts as a risk factor in the elderly.

Some people choose a form of passive suicide by refusing to eat or take medication, bringing about serious complications for their health (or, for instance, if the person is an insulin-dependent diabetic, she may decide not to use her insulin injection, aware of the hazardous consequences).

It is also important to keep in mind that the reasons old people have to end their lives are varied. Suicide increases with age and so suicide rates in the elderly are higher than in other age groups. Among the vital events that trigger a suicidal act in the elderly are the loss of a partner (especially in men), financial problems, lack of family and social support, mental health problems and alcohol-related disorders. Increasing infirmity and a loss of health, with a sense of impending helplessness, are contributory factors, particularly if there is no immediate, or foreseeable, caring network available.

Since depression is present in a great number of people who commit suicide, an early diagnosis and timely treatment of this condition could help to prevent suicide. What is more, if non-suicidal depression is not treated adequately and in good time, it may become suicidal depression. We can never insist enough when it comes to warning about the atypical nature of depression in the elderly (for more information see Chapter 6).

Obviously, depression diagnoses may become more frequent if the likelihood of this condition is not ignored. So prescribing an anti-depressive treatment for a few weeks for patients with less typical or atypical depression can be very useful. More effective psychotherapeutic techniques include an interview with diagnostic and therapeutic purposes. In such cases it is important to take the role of listener and ask for clarification when a topic is not clear enough. This may have a positive effect on old people who may perceive that their mood is being taken seriously.

No matter what a therapist's age is, old people tend to see him or her as a protective figure, as long as a relationship of trust and respect is established. For this reason, it is important to allow the patient to express freely all his feelings and emotions, no matter how embarrassing they may seem to the individual. When an old person reproaches himself or herself because '...having been a person as I used to be and to be crying now...', it is important to help the person understand that for most of the time, comparisons do not help much.

As with other age groups, the therapist should always explore whether there are suicidal thoughts present and, in case there are, they should be discussed with the patient to see whether there is a plan and to find out which reasons the individual has to continue living. When the individual has no reasons to live, hospitalization should be recommended to provide treatment and emotional support, to instil hope in the individual and to help the suicidal crisis disappear.

Because hearing difficulties may be present, it is important to speak clearly and check that what is being said is understood.

Another important aspect of the psychotherapeutic treatment of potentially suicidal elderly people is explaining to them the benefits of treatment with anti-depressive drugs, when they are supposed to start feeling better, possible adverse reactions of the medication and the frequency of follow-up appointments, which at the beginning should be at least once a week.

It is a mistake to think that elderly people do not wish to continue living on account of their age. A psychotherapeutic task for the therapist is to establish a daily routine to keep the individual busy with activities that are of interest to him.

If the elderly person has children, a valid strategy is to discuss his or her responsibility as an elder in the broader familial or social context.

Very often people suffer from several conditions that need different medical treatments. It is obligatory to check their medication regimes to avoid the use of drugs that can have a depressing effect and to ensure that their intake of psychotropic medication is not having an adverse effect on their general everyday health. As with all mental health crises, it is vital that all those involved communicate with each other, particularly when different healthcare professionals and care workers are involved.

Another measure that can be effective in the psychotherapeutic treatment of the suicidal crisis in the elderly is family counselling. In families where there is good understanding and respect among different generations, the prognosis tends to be better than in families where it is not so. The extent to which ageing and the elderly are accepted is paramount. In families where elderly people are venerated as a source of wisdom, sensibility and serenity, the prognosis is really good, while it is quite the opposite in households where old people are neglected or even maltreated.

An astute therapist may diagnose elderly abuse when old patients have visible physical damage and the explanations given by their relatives about the lesions are vague, imprecise or contradictory; when there is a long lapse of time between the time of lesion and the time of seeking medical care; and when after several appointments the elderly patient does not have any real improvement in spite of having appropriate treatment. All these manifestations suggest elderly abuse that might lead to suicidal behaviour in this period of life.

One of the most salient characteristics of the elderly considering suicide is how rigid they may have become in their thinking and how restrictive their emotional responses may consequently become. This tunnel vision often restricts alternative solutions, so it is important to explain clearly any suggested alternatives to enable those alternatives to be perceived as viable.

## HELPING THE SURVIVORS

A sudden death is a shock for those who continue to live. The magnitude of this shock depends very much on the way of dying, especially if the death is violent. It has been said that a person who commits suicide places his psychological skeleton in the emotional wardrobe of the survivors. The psychological pain following suicide can be excruciating for the survivors and can also bring social difficulties, given the cultural taboo that suicide has. If the suicide occurs in the family home, or a family member or friend finds the person, the process can be traumatic.

Suicide is the cause of death that creates the greatest culpability, hostility and stigmatization. Therefore, when facing the suicide's family, the therapist should:

- keep in mind the degree of shock and the immediate resources available for the family's emotional support

- look out for feelings of guilt or responsibility for what has happened

- elicit any suicidal thoughts, threats or similar behaviours in the dead person's relatives

- help family members recognize that the suicide was not their failure but acknowledge that the original residual distress within a family context may remain.

We are beginning to recognize that grief following suicide and assisted suicide is complicated and may be extreme in its manifestations, such that survivors show the symptoms of post-traumatic stress disorder.

In the first phase of shock, there is marked sadness among close family members. This shock phase may be followed by anger, which may be directed at anyone: the doctor, the person who died, other family members and the self. This may be followed by a guilt phase characterized by anguish for not having foreseen the event or dealt with the suicide's unsatisfied longings, and by recurrent thoughts about unresolved disputes in the relationship with the dead person, probable motives that might have contributed to the fatal end, and remembrances of the deceased.

The situation can be confused initially by denial that the death was a suicide, and with that denial comes a repressions of feelings. One way of coping may be to withdraw from social contacts. Another may be to work more hours. Another is to abuse alcohol or other substances. If, as we suggest, the suicide occurs in a milieu where there is already a restricted repertoire of managing distress, then a suicide is another event that prolongs that underlying distress. This entails a family or systemic perspective on the suicide. The problem does not end with one death.

Children in a family are particularly affected. Such events are confusing. A child may see herself as responsible for the death and needs to be included in the grieving process. Adolescents too have to come to terms with loss at a time when their emotional lives may be in turmoil.

Pain and sorrow need to be expressed in a caring context. It is at this time that the greatest emotional support should be offered to those who were most closely related to the suicide. In the days following the suicide, the focus should be on the family to establish the differences between expected and unexpected deaths, as in the case of suicide, so that family members understand how devastating this kind of death can be for the survivors. One of the aims is to prevent another suicide – that is, to prevent any one of them from making the rest of the family go through the same traumatic experience they are experiencing at present again.

Suicides do not occur in isolation. Although the person may have isolated herself, the immediate family probably still has a social network. Friends, colleagues and members of the wider family and community need to be involved and can provide a support network. What the wider community can do is to listen carefully and allow the survivors to talk about their loss. In addition, given that the grieving process is also about loss and anger, it is also important to allow for the expression of negative feelings. When a problem has been hidden in a family, a family friend or trusted family member can explain to others in the family circle that a problem has existed, maybe for years, but has been hidden from them. If professional help is necessary, it is a family member or friend who can suggest this and bring it about.

Following any death, there are formal arrangements that have to be made with the local authorities, and friends and family can help with these too.

## Guilt

The feelings of guilt that survivors often experience can be managed according to the degree of responsibility the family felt that they had over the life of the person who died. So, if suicide was committed by an individual without any responsibility or only partial responsibility over their lives at the moment of dying, it should be explained to family members that guilt is a phase many of us go through when a loved one dies, no matter what causes the person's death. We ask ourselves whether we could have done anything better or differently that may have helped. This is normal. There are some mental health problems, such as the one that the deceased suffered with, that might have resulted in the suicidal act occurring even earlier. That death did not happen before is, to a great extent, thanks to the care and attention provided by the family.

If the deceased was entirely responsible for his life, the family can be helped to understand that some people can be their own, and most dangerous, enemies. Despite our best efforts, the decision to die is out of our hands. It is important, however, to discover the circumstances that led to the death, simply to discover any underlying and continuing distress and prevent any further precipitate action by another family member. At such a time of crisis, a family may be particularly amenable to discussing their distress and negotiating another means of distress resolution.

## Imitation

The imitative effect of suicidal behaviour has long been recognized. A family history of suicidal behaviour should always be regarded as a risk factor. It is therefore important to talk to the survivors and ask directly who else is suffering. It may well be that other family members have previously attempted suicide or have a history of mental health problems.

# THE PROCESS OF NEGOTIATING DISTRESS

Meanings and their consequent actions are woven into episodes as narratives that explain daily life. Stories are the basic explanatory medium for conveying meaning. People try to use them when they encounter their practitioner, and it is stories that we scientists tell each other to illustrate our own ideas and theories away from the lecture platform. Yet meanings have to be tested in further action; they are open to challenge. 'Why did she do it?' is a basic narrative question and at the core of a thousand stories. Each story will be different but within each culture there will be rules for articulating that story and to whom it can be told. Therefore, if culture is that which underlies shared behaviour, and it is based on meanings and rules that are negotiated, then it is a process that is active and subject to change. Human nature cannot be understood from one point of view. It is necessary to have different approaches to understanding the world.

The people involved in the situation are the best source of information because they locate their knowledge in their personal and relevant contexts. A criticism of research into depression is that few people have asked the sufferers what it is like to be depressed and what works. The same goes for suicidal behaviour.

We cannot help but be touched by the stories of those that we hear. How do we deal with hopelessness in our own lives? Ignoring this question only builds a distance between ourselves and the people we are supposed to be helping. Indeed, it is the existential question of life's meaning and the effectiveness of our own agency that is perhaps central to the treatment dilemma in suicidal behaviour. For example, patients contact their general practitioners, yet they fail to discuss their suicidal feelings. Rather than categorize this as a feature of those who come to us in distress, perhaps we may have to reflect upon how we conspire not to discuss such matters. Given the incidence of suicidal behaviour among members of the medical profession, there may indeed be a common question that both patient and doctor are asking that neither can answer.

When people talk about their problems and the ensuing distress, causality is relational, events are located within episodes and sequences, and changes are being sought. Indeed, the language of distress is varied and has implications for intimate relationships. Trying to resolve conflict without an understanding of social context may mean that some persons are asked to live with raised thresholds of distress.

Instead of asking the question 'Why?', we ask the participants 'What happens?' To reduce distress we must understand those who are distressed and the ramifications of this understanding for their, and our, actions. What we have to face up to is that our tactics of distress management, if they do not match up with those of the other person, may contribute to the escalation of distress.

## CHAPTER 11

# THE INTERNET

## New Possibilities, Problems and Challenges in the Prevention of Suicide

The Internet has made a tremendous contribution to communications and has brought about new possibilities and new ways of interaction among its users that did not exist in the past.

At present, through the Internet, people who have access to this technology can communicate with their loved ones, friends and acquaintances who are far away. It is possible to chat or take part in forums to express opinions. The Internet has globalized communication with its greater outreach than traditional mass media. If used in a reasonable, appropriate and intelligent way, everything that is reasonable, appropriate and intelligent can be globalized. If, on the contrary, it is used for morbid and mean aims, then morbidity and meanness will be globalized.

The Internet offers new possibilities for suicide prevention, and several organizations disseminate their viewpoints about avoiding this cause of death. Healthcare professionals use the Internet for consultations and interventions in suicidal crisis situations with satisfactory results. Online psychiatry congresses also use this medium to discuss psychiatric emergencies, including suicide, and interventions.

The most outstanding health organizations around the world have web pages dedicated to research on suicide and its prevention, as well as electronic journals and bulletins that publish on this topic.

However, not all is wine and roses. The first manifestations of suicide through the Internet took place in the late 1990s, and they have increased significantly in several countries. The term *cybersuicide* refers precisely to suicide committed by people resulting from a challenge or information on the topic obtained via the Internet.

Media reporting of suicide is known to influence suicidal behaviour, particularly the choice of method used (Hawton and van Herringen 2009). The influence of the Internet on suicidal behaviour is less well understood, although it is an increasingly popular source of information, especially for people confronting embarrassing issues such as mental illness. Concerns have been raised about the existence of sites that promote suicide. Some people have been encouraged to use suicide as a problem-solving strategy by suicide web forums. Suicide sites are also claimed to have facilitated suicide pacts among strangers who have met and then planned their suicide through the Internet. It is possible to find out about suicide methods in detail, and particularly about obtaining medication through the Internet, via chat rooms and discussion boards.

Although dedicated suicide sites appear most frequently, there are as many sites trying to prevent suicide.

Information on methods is not the only way that the Internet can contribute to suicidal behaviour. Contributors to chat rooms may exert peer pressure to commit suicide, and idolize those who have completed suicide. We also see this in the phenomenon of facilitating suicide pacts. In these chat room discussions, any doubts or fears of people who are uncertain about suicide are reduced. Although young people writing to these chat rooms are often initially ambivalent, their resolve may strengthen as others encourage them. Withdrawing from this contact with the seemingly like-minded, or seeking help, becomes more difficult.

Since 2006 it has been illegal in Australia to use the Internet to promote or provide practical details about suicide, and Internet service providers worldwide have followed to block specific sites. A positive move has been made to maximize the likelihood that suicidal people access helpful sites in times of crisis.

## The Internet community and the coalition of the disaffected

While a sense of belonging may be possible through the Internet, one of the difficulties is virtual groups that bring about a coalition of the disaffected. While these groupings, sometimes referred to as communities, have similar interests, their disaffections are also disembodied. Usually when we express our distress, there is someone real that we are communicating with. In that communication, we gain feedback through a number of sensory modalities about how our communication is being perceived. We are regulated directly through such a social contact. We know if we are overstepping the mark through how the other person responds in a variety of ways. This is not possible through the Internet. Not only do we know whether the other person is indeed who they say they are, we have no idea of their intention because the communication modality is limited; that is, it is textual. We miss out on those changes in tone of voice, facial expression, gesture and other bodily expressions that are the very stuff of interpersonal communication. Likewise, through using only textual communication, it is easy to overstep the social mark of communication without realizing the extreme effect such texts have on the other person. The mediation of personal contact is removed.

The two young men in the Colombine massacre were avid gamers and spent much of their time online, having had difficulties becoming socially integrated with their peers. Their plans were made online with each other. Much bullying now also takes place online and is called *cyberbullying*. The anonymity of the perpetrators, and the distance between the act of bullying and its effects, both physically and emotionally, mean that previous social mediation of such acts, difficult enough in the real world, is now more difficult in a synthetic world.

In 2011, a man from the United States of America, posing as a female nurse, was given a prison sentence after he helped persuade an English man and a Canadian woman to commit suicide. The man was obsessed with suicide and hanging, and sought out people on the Internet to whom he gave advice and encouragement, while posing as a female nurse, so that they would commit suicide. He admitted to having taken part in online chats about suicide with up to 20 people and had entered into fake suicide pacts with about ten of them, five of whom were believed to have killed themselves. His plea in mitigation was that he could invoke his right to freedom of speech in communicating with other people on the Internet.

In these instances we have people invoking the rights of citizens within a society, and using 'social networks' on the Internet that have little to do with actual, everyday social contact between persons as living beings. These cybercontacts are unidimensional and, unregulated by real human contact, fall outside any ethical framework. In essence, people become disaffected, literally dislocated emotionally from their social milieu. While contact with others can be realized online, this synthetic contact is with an avatar, a computer-generated identity. When people come together for a positive purpose on a social network, they are already socialized and have incorporated the mores of the community in which they live as individuals before they join. This differentiates them from networks where the participants have no such commitment to a community.

## Suicide pacts

A 26-year-old American planned a collective suicide on 14 February, Saint Valentine's Day, using the Internet. The police arrested Gerald Krien, the promoter of the collective suicide, on a charge of soliciting aggravated murder. He was attempting to convince at least 32 North Americans to take their lives simultaneously. Krien was denounced to the police by a woman who at first had accepted an invitation to join the collective suicide but was then terrified by the confession of another participant who was considering killing her two sons before killing herself.

Collective suicide episodes using the Internet were initially reported in Japan and then spread to other countries. Although originally considered suicide pacts, they do not meet the traditional criteria: mutual agreement between two or more people to die together, at the same time, usually in the same place and by the same method. Previously it was older people with solid, affective bonds, such as spouses, family members and members of the same political organization or religious sect who made such agreements.

In the case of cybersuicides, the participants did not have any affective bond among themselves, most of them did not know the others, they had never seen one another and they did not share any common stories before getting in touch through the Internet. Some were in different places at the time of committing suicide, while others only met for the first and last time to commit collective suicide.

Formerly, the relationship between the victims of a suicide pact was typically exclusive to a couple and isolated from others. The immediate trigger for a suicide pact is often a threat to the continuity of the relationship: either the impending death of one of the individuals due to an incurable disease or the banishment of one person in a forbidden relationship.

Suicide pacts have also been associated with a rare psychiatric disorder called *folie à deux*. In this condition, two people share the same beliefs and withdraw from society. As in the case of some suicide pacts in which one person incites the other, in a *folie à deux* one person is dominant in the relationship and impresses that idea on the other. While suicide pacts are usually carried out between spouses, *folies à deux* are more common among sisters.

Internet pacts are made predominantly between people who come from highly developed countries. The people involved in such a pact have their first contact through the Internet, usually through a chat forum. These people do not have any real-life connection among themselves. There is a dominant personality that proposes the suicide pact and does all the persuasive work. This person is the one who suggests how, when and where the collective suicide will take place. In collective suicides, the people taking part may be geographically very far apart. Adolescents and young people of both sexes take part in this form of suicide.

We have to face the new challenges posed by suicide pacts on the Internet. The Internet itself is neutral. How it is used in terms of social networking is being increasingly questioned. As this book is being written, social networking has been used throughout the Middle East in the cause of democracy to liberate people in various countries. Simultaneously, in London, England, social networking was used on several days to coordinate looting and rioting by gangs, to inform police and citizens about trouble spots, and later to coordinate community action to clean up the damage from the days before. Information will seek to be free, but how we use that information is a reflection of how civilized our communities are and the moral responsibility of those involved.

In order to lessen the occurrence of Internet suicide pacts, and suicide generally, we recommend that the following measures be considered:

- Increase communication between family members by ensuring there are daily occasions when they can talk directly to each other.

- Build parent–child relationships based on affection and personal achievement, not only on the meeting of material needs, with an emphasis on belonging to a community of intimates.

- Monitor the Internet websites visited by children and adolescents. If they are in contact with forums related to death and incitement to suicide, ask for professional help urgently.

- Publish the risk factors for suicide on the Internet.

- Publish the protective factors for the prevention of suicide on the Internet.

- Publish the myths and evidence concerning suicide on the Internet.

- Publish the warning signs of a suicidal crisis on the Internet.

- Publish sources of help on the Internet about mental health and suicide that people can turn to at times of crisis.

- Publish information on the Internet about groups in cyberspace that pose a risk in relation to suicide.

- Publish simple steps that will enable people to act if faced with someone in a suicide crisis – for example, to ask if he has considered suicide and, if so, to ensure he does not have access to anything he may use to harm himself and that he is not left alone until the crisis is over.

- Each country should legislate against those who incite suicide.

- Be aware of cyberbullying. If this is happening to your child take it extremely seriously. It is not simply a synthetic phenomenon occurring in cyberspace, the consequences are real for your child – and you.

## Chapter 12

# RECOMMENDATIONS FOR A SUICIDE PREVENTION STRATEGY

Suicide rates have increased worldwide and suicide is among the three leading causes of death among those aged 15–44 years in some countries. It is also the second leading cause of death in the 10–24 years age group. Suicide attempts are 20 times more frequent than completed suicide. Although suicide rates have been highest among the male elderly, we now see increasing rates among young people such that they are now the group at highest risk in many countries.

Strategies involving restriction of access to common methods of suicide, such as firearms or toxic substances like pesticides, have proved to be effective in reducing suicide rates; however, there is a need to adopt multi-agency approaches involving many levels of intervention and activities.

## INTERNATIONAL AND NATIONAL INITIATIVES

Worldwide, the prevention of suicide has not been adequately addressed. Because there is a lack of awareness of suicide as a major problem and because of the taboo in many cultures against discussing suicide openly, few countries prioritize suicide prevention. What complicates suicide prevention is that it is not simply a healthcare problem; it requires a comprehensive approach, including departments of health and education, religious and legal bodies, politicians and the media.

There are various initiatives worldwide to prevent suicide. Many of these are involved in removing the causes of distress and the means of achieving suicide.

Depression and alcohol-use disorders are a major risk factor for suicide in those countries where alcohol is allowed. There is compelling evidence indicating that adequate prevention and treatment of depression and alcohol and substance abuse can reduce suicide rates (Hawton and van Heeringen 2009), as does follow-up contact with those who have attempted suicide.

The World Health Organization suggests measures to prevent suicide:

- Provide support and treatment to populations at risk – people with depression, the elderly, young people – and provide better treatment for mental ill health.

- Reduce the availability of, and access to, means of suicide, including the detoxification of motor vehicle fumes and domestic gas and additional controls of toxic substances. Provide sustainable surveillance of pesticide poisoning. Improve the medical management and mental healthcare of people with pesticide poisoning, providing training to develop or strengthen community programmes that minimize risks of intentional and unintentional pesticide poisoning.

- Support and strengthen networks for the survivors of suicide.

- Improve training for primary healthcare workers and healthcare professionals, particularly in the fields of mental health.

- Minimize sensationalist news in the mass media.

Some countries have their own national strategies for suicide prevention according to their own characteristics. In England, several measures have been implemented aimed at preventing suicide: improving the diagnosis and treatment provided by general practitioners, improving mental health services to patients who suffer from depression and have a suicide risk, minimizing access to means that can be used to commit suicide, and attempting to modify public attitudes towards depression and suicide.

In Norway, there have been initiatives to improve child mental health and improve access to mental health provision in schools; improvements in general medical practice; and an improved media strategy regarding the reporting of suicide and how suicide is portrayed in film and television dramas.

Sweden has concentrated on improving public understanding of suicidal behaviour; support and treatment initiatives for people at risk; implementation of suicide prevention training programmes; and minimizing the availability of suicidal means.

For countries where prevention programmes exist, there appears to be a central core of measures:

- to provide social and medical support to people in a crisis situation

- to educate children and young people in the management of conflict

- to fight alcoholism and drug dependence

- to provide social and medical support to vulnerable groups: old people, single mothers, unemployed people, ethnic minorities, immigrants, and rural workers whose existence is challenged by a global economy

- to update primary healthcare professionals, paediatricians, teachers, priests and police officers about prevention and the identification of suicide risk factors and depression

- to minimize the availability of suicidal means such as firearms, pesticides and other toxic substances

- to ban sensationalist information about suicide in the mass media

- to treat mental diseases

- to promote multi-disciplinary conferences about suicidal behaviour and the different aspects of prevention.

Some suicide prevention measures are difficult to implement in all countries. Although we recognize that people with a mental health disorder are more likely to commit suicide than the rest of the population, it is sometimes difficult for people with mental health problems to gain access to treatment. In many countries, mental health services are concentrated in the capital or the largest cities, the cost of specialized care is high, and the individuals cannot afford drugs for follow-up and maintenance. The difficulties may be further confounded by a reluctance openly to discuss problems of mental health; having psychiatric problems is stigmatized and the subject of suicide is taboo.

A similar situation takes place when attempts are made to ban sensationalist news in the mass media. Powerful economic interests are behind the lucrative business of reporting human suffering in a sensationalist way. The exploitation of human tragedy as entertainment is a central feature of 24-hour, seven-days-a-week news channels.

## Problems for indigenous peoples

The problems that young people face and that place them at risk are amplified for indigenous peoples. When children are abused, they may see their mothers being abused and live in a household where drugs or alcohol are misused. Young people in these communities may feel themselves both victimized and unsafe, which leads them to take their own lives. Poverty is endemic and there are high levels of unemployment. For urban youth, there are weakening social bonds and an ingrained historical and cultural trauma related to colonization and racism. Poverty, violence and alcohol abuse are a dangerous cocktail. In the Montana-Wyoming Tribal Leaders Association health, mental health and social services are integrated to keep children alive and in school. Projects are aimed at teaching students how to help each other. Changing the culture at school is also important, which includes countering bullying, encouraging self-discipline and finding ways to deal with behavioural problems. There are also training programmes for teachers.

# A COMPREHENSIVE NATIONAL PROGRAMME

We suggest the following initiatives for a comprehensive national programme for the prevention of suicide. It is important to keep in mind that multi-agency programmes are always fraught with difficulty, and a lot of perseverance will be required. Suicide is a preventable cause of death in many cases. Many lives can be saved, even with limited resources, if simple measures are taken. Interagency coordination is central and vital; it is also probably the biggest stumbling block, so any initiatives will require recognized leadership. Preventing suicide is not restricted to the realm of psychiatrists, psychologists and other professionals and needs to engage a broad platform of community leaders and educational institutions.

## Interagency initiatives

- Improve services for people in a suicidal crisis with a coordinated system of health and social care provision. This will mean a multi-disciplinary task force for mental health emergencies that will coordinate mental health services and refer people with a high suicide risk for specialized treatment or hospitalization.

- Improve the recognition of depression and emphasize the problems of alcohol abuse.

- Start suicide prevention actions prioritizing the reduction of suicides by adolescents and children, since those actions tend to get full support from the community.

- Hold scientific events for the exchange of experiences among people interested in the prevention of suicide.

## Educational initiatives

- Deliver lectures for doctors, nurses and social workers who work in general hospitals about topics such as suicide myths, the exploration of suicidal ideas, suicide risk groups, the diagnosis and treatment of depression in adolescents and the elderly, suicidal risk evaluation and major measures to prevent suicide during a suicidal crisis.

- Offer lectures in schools addressed to students, teachers and the family about interesting and understandable topics so that the audience can have a better understanding of suicide and its prevention.

- Carry out early interventions in situations where a suicide has been completed to prevent the imitative effects of that behaviour, mainly in schools.

- Stop bullying! Bullying is not a single-person phenomenon; it is a whole-school phenomenon that reaches out into the family and the community. Cyberbullying is on the increase and is a potent source of distress in adolescents and children.

- Promote activities that reinforce self-discipline and self-esteem, and encourage a variety of ways to solve problems.

## Community initiatives

- Collaborate with religious organizations and community groups to identity people at risk, to offer educational and support programmes and to remove the stigma associated with mental health.

- Pay immediate attention to the suicide's relatives and other survivors to help them grieve normally. Survivors can become efficient participants in self-help groups.

- Foster the formation and education of groups of volunteers in the community and establish a helpline to provide support to suicidal people with the participation of professionals and volunteers with an aptitude for this task.

## Media initiatives

- Gain the support of the mass media to produce radio and television programmes and newspaper articles about suicide and suicide prevention.

- Suggest workshops to discuss how to deal with the topic of suicide in the media.

## The Cuban six-level approach

In Cuba, the National Program for the Prevention of Suicide started in 1989 with three main objectives: to avoid the first suicide attempt; to avoid the repetition of attempted suicide; and to prevent completed suicide. This programme comprises six levels of support: the family doctor, the polyclinic, the hospital, the municipality, the province and the nation. Each level has its own task, but the family doctor in primary healthcare is the main actor with the participation of community leaders, formal and informal, institutions and organizations.

## SOME FINAL THOUGHTS

Preventing suicidal behaviour is a complex undertaking. The concept of suicide exists in all cultures and it is unlikely that we can eliminate related behaviours that have existed over the centuries. Suicide is complex, and psychological, social, biological, cultural and environmental factors are involved.

The problems of suffering and distress are universal to humankind and are at the core of world religions as well as medical initiatives. While we cannot take away suffering and distress, we can help people to be resilient and to cope with suffering and distress as they do with physical pain. We can help mitigate anguish following loss, relieve helplessness in the face of disaster, and counteract hopelessness and doubt in the face of catastrophe. In terms of prevention, we need to promote a variety of ways of managing distress. Indeed, as human beings we need to learn how to suffer as well as to achieve ease, comfort and happiness.

The World Health Organization is concerned that suicide is a leading cause of death worldwide. As self-inflicted death is one of the three leading causes of death for young people under 25, we need to ask what can be done to save thousands of people from such violent death. If deaths from suicide comprise more than half of the violent deaths in the world, and that includes more than the deaths we see in war and street killing, then we need to make serious social interventions.

Suicide may be a healthcare problem in its widest sense, but it cannot simply be medicalized. To do so ignores the complexity of the problem. We know that depression plays a major role and that is this is also linked to economic circumstances. Similarly, we know that in rural cultures like South India, where farmers are victims of a globalized economy, culture plays a part in the methods people choose to kill themselves. It is the male head of the family, the breadwinner, who is killing himself. But culture also has an economic aspect too. The method chosen for death is pesticide poisoning. We cannot say that this is simply a mental disorder and ignore the agrarian crisis. If we offer aid in the form of pesticides to improve crop yields for farmers in the name of development, we need to rethink this strategy in the economic light of a globalized economy if those same farmers are using that very pesticide to kill themselves because the market fails to provide an income for their families.

Unmitigated distress is the central feature of suicidal behaviour. We cannot simply lay this distress at the door of personal health. We become distressed in a community that includes others. Those communities are also located within a wider economic setting. Any interventions will need to be complex, but we have argued that empowering people to have more control over their own health will be an important step in improving their mental health. However, the hopelessness of unemployment and the despair of poverty cannot be ignored.

Families manage their distress. Sometimes a community will support them, and these ties are important. However, it is the family members that recognize amongst themselves who is complaining, who is unhappy, who is becoming withdrawn. Given a little help and understanding, it is the family that can provide the necessary psychological and emotional resources to prevent those violent deaths that tear them apart.

In many countries we see a proportion of the population that is disaffected and alienated, with no ties to society. Some of these people take part in antisocial and sometimes aggressive behaviour. Others turn that aggression upon themselves. The question remains how we encourage those societal ties. Pérez emphasizes the concept of responsibility, not only for individual behaviour, but also the responsibilities we have as parents, as friends, as therapists and as communities. We cannot simply transfer the responsibility from one to another; we have to set the example ourselves by taking responsibility both for our own actions and for those of others.

Appendix 1

# A MODEL OF THE SYSTEMIC MANAGEMENT OF DISTRESS

Suicidal behaviour is seen as a strategy for coping with distress within the family group. Family or small groups are stressed by developmental or life-cycle changes where substances may be used to reduce, manage or avoid conflict. Challenging behaviour is a communicative process expressing a challenging situation that reflects the family system as a whole and is often an attempt to manage the rate of change in a family. Families organize themselves to manage developmental crises in varying ways. Some families accommodate change easily and naturally without excessive levels of distress. Some families develop within their own cultural tradition a means of accommodating change that involves hostility and conflict, leading to high levels of distress. Indeed, some families use substances quite legitimately to regulate distress. In this way, alcohol and substance abuse is not necessarily a genetic problem in families, but is an accepted way of self-medicating distress. This works at a cultural level too where some substances are classified as dangerous, yet alcohol is accepted. Nevertheless, in many areas of the world, alcohol consumption is seen as a significant contributory factor in suicidal behaviour. What we suggest here is that it is the use of alcohol as a failing attempt to resolve distress that becomes the problem. Similarly, we have an armamentarium of psychoactive substances, culturally validated and professionally prescribed for resolving distress, but these too become problematic when the distress for which they are prescribed is not resolved.

Aldridge's model (Figure A.1) proposes a way of understanding the systemic management of distress. This model can be applied to systemic distress with reference to the individual, to a family or to an organization. The singular criterion is, 'Is distress reduced: yes or no?' It is unresolved distress that is causative and as we will see, if strategies to resolve that distress fail, then distress escalates. For example, a headache may be resolved by taking an aspirin. A stronger headache may need two aspirins. A hundred aspirins would not be an improvement.

We start simply with the occurrence of a crisis. In Figure A.1 we see that a developmental crisis is recognized in a family (a). Something happens. A life event occurs. This event can be a change in blood pressure, a viral infection, a personal disappointment or an argument with a partner. Something happens that constitutes an 'event' that is distressing, the consequences of which must be resolved.

As an adaptation to that crisis, thresholds of distress are threatened (b). Someone is upset.

There then follows a strategic move to reduce that distress (c) according to the repertoire of distress management that the individual has. Sitting down and relaxing may regulate blood pressure, the immune system may react to the virus, we may cry in frustration or retire to a quiet place. We may take a pill or imbibe a drink. Distress is reduced (d).

Our strategy of distress management works. What we propose here is that we all have a repertoire of dealing with challenging situations. This personal repertoire for relieving distress is validated (e) because it works and (f) stability is maintained.

This is a simple homeostatic loop (see Section X of Figure A.1). Change happens; we have ways of dealing with it.

However, should distress not be reduced an alternative strategy from the repertoire of distress management is used (g). We may reduce blood pressure by meditating, we can wait for a head cold to come and go, or a child may run around boisterously and shout. Maybe we take pills over a longer period of time or an extra glass of alcohol. If distress is reduced (g) then this alternative strategy is validated as a legitimate means of reducing distress (e).

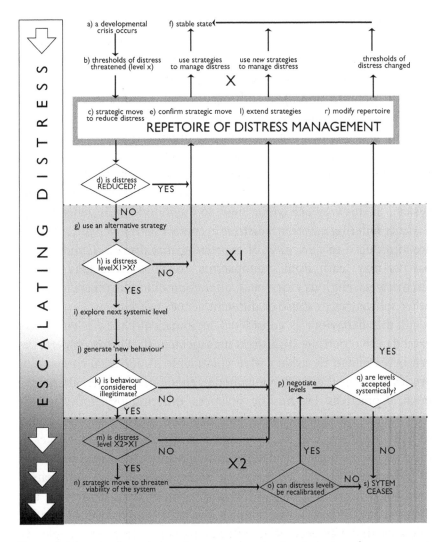

Figure A.1 Levels of escalating distress and systemic strategies of management

This also explains why substance abuse may run in families without necessarily having a genetic origin. It is simply an acceptable strategy in the repertoire of distress management that is learned. Tolerance is not simply a physiological phenomenon for the individual but also a systemic phenomenon within a family or social group.

If distress continues to escalate (h), where levels of distress are higher in X1 than in X, and systemic thresholds threaten to exceed to a point where the very viability of the system itself is threatened, distress management strategies are explored from a higher level of systemic organization (i). A shift occurs from organic to personal, or from personal to marital, marital to familial, familial to communal, communal to social, or departmental to organizational.

This strategy will depend upon the systemic rules for distress management at this contextual level and will accord to the tradition of the system – that is, the biography, memory and construing of the system. In this way behaviour 'new' to the individual is generated (j). Patients suffering emotional distress in contact with psychiatric services are introduced to new ways of expressing that distress. Children and parents may learn from grandparents, social workers may suggest alternatives, religious elders may offer counselling, drinkers may find other substances to abuse or different venues to frequent.

If this behaviour is considered legitimate (k) then it effectively extends the repertoire of distress management (l). Distress repertoires can be extended by asking what is available in our local community. We learn about the most sympathetic general practitioner, alternative medical practices, lay healing practices, differing psychotherapeutic techniques, the latest diets, exercises and alternative life styles, to alleviate distress. It must be noted here that the current level of distress may be higher than at (b) although still within the boundaries of tolerable distress. In this way, some systems live with raised levels of distress: learning to live with pain, anxiety, depression and delinquency. Indeed, some families live with a high level of conflict tolerance that may become accepted as everyday life. Some people live with drinking patterns that would be unacceptable to others but are acceptable to their partners. While there are governmental guidelines about how many units of alcohol can be safely consumed each week, these 'social' thresholds may be regularly transgressed.

The current level of distress may not fall to the initial level (m). The system then calibrates itself to accommodate a higher level of distress. Distress at X2 is still greater than at X. When this occurs, a family then becomes a family system with a symptom carrier – for example diabetic, asthmatic, problematic, anorectic, epileptic, tense, depressed, delinquent or alcoholic – who expresses her symptoms at times of distress to maintain family stability. Not only is the repertoire of distress management extended (l) but also the initial thresholds of distress (b) are altered. The system returns itself to a stable state (f), but that state is altered. Distress is endemic to the family system and becomes a way of relating. Perhaps more significantly, physiological tolerance is so altered within the individual that physical addiction occurs.

If distress levels escalate such that systemic viability is further threatened, an overt strategic move is made to threaten the viability of the system (n). This move will be one which is culturally approved and based upon the systemic tradition of manifesting distress – for example, blood sugar levels escalate into diabetes and then a diabetic coma, essential hypertension becomes raised and develops into a stroke, delinquent behaviours escalate into challenging episodes of physical contact and abuse, or strategies of medication escalate into self-poisoning or alcoholic coma.

When a system becomes so threatened, it is necessary to implement measures to reduce distress and maintain systemic viability. This will be observed in the behavioural strategies used in a crisis. The vital question is whether thresholds of distress can be recalibrated (o). For some physiological levels this may not be physically possible and the patient dies. For other psychological levels, this calibration may mean a continuing psychotic episode or perceptual outbursts of anger. For some social situations there is withdrawal, hospitalization and temporary estrangement.

Should these crisis strategies fail and the systemic thresholds be exceeded then the system will cease (s). Someone dies, leaves or is forcibly removed.

On the other hand, a crisis may be successfully negotiated (p) and an attempt made to recalibrate the systemic thresholds of distress and change systemic construing (q). Thresholds of distress are then changed within the repertoire of distress management (r). Should the negotiation of such systemic change not be successfully validated throughout the system, to the satisfaction of all members, the system will cease (s). In this way we see that people leave families by death, leave marriages by divorce, become expelled from school, are sacked from an organization and discharged from hostels. At the organic level, livers are ruined or brains damaged.

In this model, using a substance can be seen as a means of promoting change and maintaining stability. But substance use may also promote further conflict, and levels of distress are tolerated at a level higher than the initial level. Substance use then becomes abuse and can itself become a life-event threatening stability. Throughout this model, strategic moves that attempt to reduce distress and recalibrate the system may themselves act reflexively as 'life events', which in their turn have to be accommodated. Having a drink or taking a pill may work at first. When this becomes the only means of resolving distress, it then becomes a problem. This process is known as iatrogenesis; treatment itself becomes the cause of further problems and adverse effects. We see this in chronic pain patients, when pain medication becomes the only solution and may result in substance abuse. The problem here is that when another strategy is suggested, like a psychological intervention, the previously prescribed medication is used as an overdose in suicidal behaviour.

Our simple plea here is that we encourage people through education and healthcare initiatives to widen their strategies for the management of distress. This involves promoting resilience, tolerating difficulties and resolving conflict through negotiation.

# APPENDIX 2

# GLOSSARY OF TERMS

**Accidental suicide** refers to death resulting from a suicidal attempt using a highly lethal method or death caused by complicating factors in the method used. In neither case does the individual intend their actions to result in death.

**Acute stressors** are factors common to all human beings that can precipitate a suicidal act in some individuals. Among the most common ones are relational conflicts, punishment or reprimands by parents of their adolescent children, loss of a significant relationship, or an impending court appearance or criminal prosecution.

**Altruistic suicide** is a suicide that is seemingly committed for the benefit of others by a person who is strongly integrated into society. Some people see it as a duty to commit suicide when they feel that they are becoming a burden to others. An heroic suicide may occur, for example, when a mother puts herself in the way of car to save her child from injury or a policeman dies in the line of duty.

**Amplified (extended) suicide** refers to cases where the suicidal individual takes the lives of others who do not wish to die. An individual may induce the suicide of a group of people or may cause the death of several relatives but may not die himself due to unforeseeable circumstances or failure of the method chosen.

**Anomic suicide** is triggered by a person's inability to cope with sudden and unfavourable change in a situation, resulting in disillusionment, disappointment and death. People feel that they have nothing more to lose, being alienated from the culture in which they live.

**Apparent suicide** is a death probably caused by suicide.

**Assisted suicide** refers to a suicide in which the person dies voluntarily aided by another person. The suicidal person is advised about how to commit suicide and is provided with suicidal means and instructed on their use. The practice varies in its legality or legitimacy depending upon the culture in which it occurs. The primary aim is that people have more control over end-of-life decisions, to alleviate suffering as the end of life draws near. Campaigns for assisted suicide emphasize greater choice for the individual and access to a range of medical and palliative services providing terminally ill people with the option of a painless, assisted death.

**Attitudes towards suicide** are opinions, criteria, feelings and behaviours towards suicide as a way of dying and those who think of it, attempt it or complete it. These attitudes are culture-bound and, as a rule, are grouped into two categories: punitive and permissive. Punitive attitudes view death by suicide as a sign of cowardice, a sin, and an act that must be punished. Permissive attitudes, on the other hand, view suicide as an individual's right, an act of courage, a sign of personal freedom, a heroic act that is ethically acceptable.

**Biological theory about suicide** arises from intensive studies of the psychobiology of suicide over recent decades. Suicidal behaviour is characterized by a disorder associated with serotonergic neurotransmission and endocrine functions, particularly cortisol and tyrotrophine secretion. It is believed that suicidal people have low concentrations of serotonin in certain areas of the brain and low blood cholesterol concentrations, especially in the O type blood group. These findings are not conclusive. Low levels of 5-hydroxyindoleacetic acid (5-HIAA), a serotonin metabolite, and low blood concentrations of homovanillic acid (HVA), a dopamine metabolite, have been found in the cerebrospinal fluid (CSF) of suicide attempters. Some researchers consider HVA a more effective predictor than 5-HIAA. Low activity of the platelet monoamine oxidase enzyme has been found in people who have made self-annihilation attempts, and suicidal behaviour has been associated with the hypothalamus-hypophysis-suprarenal axis, since abnormally high cortisol concentration has been found prior to a suicidal attempt, as well as abnormal dexamethasone suppression test results in 60 per cent of depressed suicidal people compared with depressed non-suicidal people. The hypothalamus-hypophysis-suprarenal axis has also been implicated in self-destructive behaviour, as have other hormones. A significant decrease of testosterone has been observed in people who commit suicide by violent methods.

**Bleeding** or exsanguination is a method by which the person cuts herself, usually an artery, and there is a fatal drop in blood pressure.

**Caregiver** is a person who provides care for others in need.

**Centre for Suicide Prevention** is an institution for the treatment of people in suicide crisis where mental health professionals and volunteers provide different kinds of therapies that include face-to-face and telephone care.

**Chronic stressors** are factors that may predispose some individuals to commit a suicidal act, among which are the early deaths of a child's parents, divorce, family communication problems, substance abuse, sexual promiscuity, school problems, marital maladjustments, job inadaptability, unemployment, painful and/or incapacitating disease. These can be considered events that occur in an individual's life that pave the way for an acute stressor to bring about a suicidal act.

**Chronic suicidal behaviours** are behaviours that lead to the individual's self-destruction, not immediately or intentionally but in the long term, with different degrees of physical, psychic or social degeneration. Chronic suicidal behaviours include alcoholism, drug addiction, antisocial behaviours, neurotic invalidity, asceticism and martyrdom. However, these self-destructive behaviours do not share one of the main characteristics of suicide: to end a life at once. For that reason, chronic suicides are not considered real suicides by many researchers.

**Cyberbullying** is the use of Internet chat forums, social networking media, mobile phones or other devices to deliver text or images intended to hurt or embarrass another person. The persons involved in this bullying can remain anonymous and are dislocated from normal social constraints.

**Cybersuicide** is related to the influence of the Internet on the incidence of suicide in people who navigate through cyberspace, where they can find suicidal games and jokes and even music for suicides. There are opportunities to discuss suicide options for those who see suicide as a possibility for all. Suicide notes and incitement to commit suicide can be found but are becoming more rare as Internet providers assume more responsibility for content.

**Deliberate self-harm** is the name given to a suicide attempt. It is defined as an act that does not result in death but whereby an individual deliberately harms himself. It is believed that the attempt is more frequent in youths and females, and the methods most commonly used are *soft* and *non-violent*, mainly the ingestion of medication and toxic substances.

**Deliberate self-harm syndrome** is self-harming behaviour frequently found in intellectually disabled patients (and some patients with personality disorders).

**Disorder** in medicine refers to an abnormality, often of function or a disturbance. 'Mental disorder' is sometimes used as a less value-laden term than mental illness or mental disease and acknowledges the complexity of factors – biological, psychological, social and cultural – that occur in distressing human conditions.

**Double suicide** is the suicide of two very emotionally close people who may, or may not, have a suicidal pact. They can be father or mother and child, siblings or spouses.

**Drowning** is a method of suicide by deliberate submersion in water, often involving a heavy weight to avoid the body coming to the surface.

**Egoistic suicide** is a suicide related to the deterioration of social and familial bonds when the individual experiences a sense of personal meaninglessness and dissatisfaction.

**Exsanguination** (see Bleeding)

**Fatalistic suicide** is a type of suicide caused by excessive social regulation – that is, society exerts an unbearable control over most of the individual's acts when people do not want to live under an increasingly oppressive regime. The person considers himself to be doomed by fate, and death is seen as an escape from oppression. We see this in prison suicides and in some work environments.

**Fire** or immolation is a suicidal method frequently used as a protest, for example in Cuba and Sri Lanka. In certain parts of India, the ritual of *suttee* was one where a Hindu widow lay upon her husband's funeral pyre.

**Firearm** use is one of the main suicidal methods, where someone shoots himself or herself, and is a common method in the United States of America.

**First psychological aid** is a suicide crisis intervention technique that comprises the following stages: (1) Contacting the individual in crisis; (2) Identifying the problem and its characteristics; (3) Finding non-suicidal solutions; (4) Concrete actions; (5) Follow-up.

**Frustrated suicide** is a suicidal act that does not lead to the individual's death due to fortuitous, casual or unforeseeable circumstances.

**Grief** is a reaction to the death of a loved one. The grief for a suicide is characterized by stigmatization, suicidal ideas, feelings of guilt, seeking reasons why the person killed themselves and late regret for not having done enough to prevent the other person dying.

**Hanging** is one of the most common suicidal methods used by males in both urban and rural areas.

*Hara-kiri* or *seppuku* is a traditional, ritual suicide method in Japan. The individual runs a sword through his abdomen to kill himself by disembowelment. It was seen as a way of preserving one's honour and existed as a ceremonial form reserved for warriors. An attendant, who would execute the final killing sword, stroke accompanied the warrior who performed the act.

**Hope Telephone** is one of the many names given to the telephone services for crisis intervention.

**Iatrogenesis** occurs when medical or psychological treatments themselves become the cause of further problems and adverse effects.

*Inseki-jisatsu* refers to a suicide carried out by a person in order to take responsibility for another person's reproachable acts. The headlines of Japanese newspapers often reflect this phenomenon that usually involves people from high social classes, such as company presidents, politicians and school principals. *Inseki-jisatsu* may also take place in families when any of its members – children or adolescents – commit an offence that provokes social agitation. Their parents are prosecuted and some of them end their lives to show remorse. Although the actual number of deaths by *inseki-jisatsu* might be small, this type of suicide must also be prevented.

**Intentional suicide** is a suicidal act carried out by an individual with the deliberate purpose of dying.

**Interventions** are a group of techniques used to abort a suicidal crisis and relieve distress.

**Jumping** (leaping) is a method frequently used by suicides in large cities where there are accessible tall buildings.

*Karojisatsu* is the name given to suicide by hyperactivity. Its frequency is increasing in Japan. It comes from the Japanese word *karoshi* that means death resulting from overwork (more than 3000 hours every year), due to stress caused by hyperproductivity on the job.

**Lethality** is the capability of causing death. It is a consequence of several factors, such as individual susceptibility, lack of availability of immediate specialized care, and the potency or toxicity of the material used.

**Mass suicide** refers to the suicide of groups of people often motivated by religious or political reasons. Although it need not be an explicit pact, in every mass or extended suicide there is an implicit agreement among the group members to die by suicide if certain previously considered circumstances arise.

**Meaning** is the message implicit in every suicidal act that can be made sense of by means of the question, 'What for?' This question can be answered in different ways: 'To die', 'To attract other people's attention', 'To ask for help', 'To hurt other people', 'To join deceased loved ones', 'To show others the immensity of their problem', 'Not to face difficult situations', etc. It does not refer to the motive. The motive is discovered by asking the question, 'Why?'

**Mental disorder** (see Disorder)

**Methods** are the ways and means by which an individual tries to end his life. As a rule, individuals choose from among the methods that are available to them and which are culturally acceptable. Methods have been classified into *hard* or *violent* and *soft* or *non-violent*. Among the hard methods are firearms, hanging, jumping, and cutting major blood vessels. Among soft methods are substance ingestion and inhalation.

**Motive** describes the reasons a suicide attempter offers to explain his suicidal act. When a suicide has been completed, the relatives tend to speculate about the possible reasons why the person killed himself. We may also find the motive for the death written in a suicide note. The assumed motive is not necessarily the cause of the suicidal act. Among the most frequent motives are couple conflicts, a jaded love, familial disputes, humiliating reprimands to children and adolescents, the loss by death of a dear one, divorce, or a way of escaping imminent prosecution or imprisonment.

**Myths** are stories related to suicidal behaviour that are culturally accepted by, and deeply rooted in, the population but not supported by any scientific truth.

**No-suicide contract** is a pact or agreement between the therapist and the individual with a suicidal risk. The therapist's main objective is to obtain the individual's commitment not to harm himself or commit suicide by making him responsible for his own life. This kind of contract does not guarantee that the individual will not commit suicide so it should not be used with anyone who is obviously not in a condition to accomplish it.

**Oblation** is an ecclesiastical term applied to suicide marked by altruistic characteristics where the person presents himself as an offering.

**Parasuicide** is a term used mainly in Europe to refer to a suicide attempt and self-harm where there is deemed to be no apparent intention to die. These are non-fatal acts in which a person deliberately causes injury to himself or ingests an overdose of prescribed medication. Such acts are considered as serious healthcare events and are strong indicators for a later completed suicide.

**Postvention** refers to the support needed by suicide attempters and suicide relatives. It is a way of preventing further harm.

**Pre-suicidal syndrome** is a psychic state that precedes a suicidal act and is characterized by constriction of affection and the intellect, inhibition of aggressiveness, and suicidal fantasies, all of which reinforce one another. The pre-suicidal syndrome is not a component of any psychiatric disease but a common sign of disorders that can lead to suicide.

**Pseudosuicide** is a complex of behaviours that may be violent and result in injury or death. These deaths may appear as suicides. In some cases they are not intentional, are without premeditation and conscious awareness and therefore without personal responsibility. The cause may be sleep related or a disturbed reaction to toxins in the body that alter states of consciousness. This lack of personal agency separates these behaviours from suicide. Some can be the result of terrifying visual hallucinations, as happens with delirium tremens in nephritic alcoholic or hepatic ureic coma patients. Another form may appear during a psychotic episode when a person hears voices telling him to jump off a high building, throw himself in front of a train or do something extremely dangerous. The person is not able to protect herself from the potential hazards of these somatic or mental disorders. Parasomnia pseudosuicide refers to such deaths when related to sleep disorders and sleep-walking.

**Psychache** refers to unbearable psychological pain or emotional anguish that reaches intolerable intensity, emphasizing the psychological suffering of a person contemplating suicide within a matrix of emotional and relational problems. The term was first coined by Edwin Shneidman in *Suicide as Psychache: A Clinical Approach to Self-destructive Behavior* (Schneidman 1993).

**Psychological autopsy** is an investigation, following a completed suicide, carried out by means of structured and semi-structured interviews with the suicide's relatives, doctor, neighbours and friends. It aims at determining whether suicide was the cause of death, and looks at the signs that preceded the event in a retrospective reconstruction of the person's life to get a better understanding of his death. Most death certificates are inaccurate regarding suicide; for example, a death by asphyxiation due to drowning doesn't specify whether it was accidental, homicidal or suicidal. The exact mode of death may be unclear. By examining the details of the deceased person's life history, we can clarify what role the person had in her own demise.

**Rational suicide** is a term used to define suicides that take place in the absence of a mental illness, as an individual's supposed expression of freedom to choose his own death – above all, in situations in which life does not offer any opportunities, and where there is marked intentionality and a rational motivation that justify the act. Suicide can be rational, but can also be a mistake. Some suicidologists consider this term ambiguous and unrealistic, and consider that suicides without a mental health problem are very rare, that all suicides are irrational and that there is a duty of care to prevent suicidal persons from ending their own lives.

**Repeater** is an individual who has made previous suicide attempts.

**Repertoire of distress management** refers to the coping mechanisms that an individual has for managing distress. This repertoire is personal but also related to what is learnt in a family and to the cultural setting of the individual. This is the reason why we see the same behaviour, suicide, in most cultures, but some methods are more prevalent in particular cultures (like firearms in the United States, immolation in Cuba and Sri Lanka and pesticide poisoning in rural India).

**Risk factor** is a term borrowed from epidemiology, the statistical study of health events in human populations, and shows how a particular variable is associated with the likelihood that a person will have a disease. These are not causal factors, as people may possess the factor but not be suicidal. As suicide is not a disease, in the sense that there is no recognized pathogenic agent that can be identified or transmitted, these factors are observable but cannot predict suicide. However, the general risk factors for suicide are:

- a mental disorder, notably depression

- a substance-abuse disorder or alcohol-abuse disorder

- a prior suicide attempt

- a family history of the above factors

- a family history of suicide

- a history of family violence, including physical or sexual abuse

- exposure to the suicidal behaviour of others, such as family members, peers, or media figures where suicide has taken place

- access to lethal means (for example, pesticides in rural Indian communities and firearms in the United States).

These will vary according to the cultural setting.

**Samaritans** is an organization for the prevention of suicide in which volunteers trained in the art of listening counsel those in distress face-to-face or over the telephone.

*Sati* (see *Suttee* and Self-immolation)

**Self-destructive behaviour** is the name given to a group of acts carried out by an individual that can cause self-inflicted injuries, such as burning himself with cigarettes, cutting off parts of his body or committing suicidal acts.

**Self-harm behaviour** is self-destructive behaviour that causes direct tissue damage. It is not meant to cause death, and the lesions are not so extensive or severe as to cause lethal damage. When repetitive self-harm behaviour provokes tissue damage, beta-endorphins are released causing analgesia and a pleasant mood. The rewarding sensations condition the repetition of the self-harm behaviour to maintain a chronic release of endogenous opioids to continue the experience of that pleasant sensation, with lessening of the dysphoric symptoms that appear immediately after the self-harm.

**Self-help groups** are groups of patients with a common health problem who decide to work together for their well-being – for example, groups of suicide attempters and suicide survivors.

**Self-immolation** is a method of setting oneself on fire, often as a form of protest or for martyrdom. It has a long tradition in some cultures and has become a form of radical political protest.

**Self-inflicted harm** refers to the harmful effects resulting from a suicidal attempt or a suicide. It also includes the aftermath of self-destructive acts carried out by the individual without an intention to die.

**Self-mutilation** is an act by which an individual cuts off any part of his body. It need not be with suicidal purposes (see also Self-harm behaviour).

**Self-starvation** involves refusing food as a form of political protest or for the purposes of martyrdom. Like self-immolation (see above), it has a long tradition in some cultures and has become a form of radical political protest.

*Seppuku* is a ritualized suicidal method used in twelfth-century Japan. The term *hara-kiri* is also used sometimes (literally *hara*, 'belly' + *kiru*, 'cut').

**Suicidal act** refers to a suicide attempt or suicide.

**Suicidal attempt** is also known as parasuicide.

**Suicidal behaviour** is used to refer to suicidal thoughts, suicide attempts and suicide.

**Suicide by cop** is a controversial topic and occurs when a person engages in criminal behaviour, often using a firearm, with the intention that, through his own provocative behaviour, he will be shot by the police when being apprehended rather than taken into custody.

**Suicidal circumstances** are the circumstances in which a suicidal act takes place. Among them are the localization of the place (familiar, unfamiliar, far, near) where it occurred, the likelihood of being found (high, uncertain, unlikely, likely, accidental), rescue accessibility (asking for help, leaving notes or any other hints that make it possible to be found or, on the contrary, taking the necessary precautions not to be found), time needed to be found, availability of medical care.

**Suicidal communications** are classified as follows:

- *Verbal direct suicidal communication.* The individual expresses explicitly his wish to end his life: 'I will kill myself', 'I will commit suicide', 'What I have to do is to end this once and for all'.

- *Non-verbal direct suicidal communication.* Some acts indicate that a suicide is likely to take place soon – for instance, having access to suicidal methods, leaving farewell notes, or giving away valuable possessions.

- *Verbal indirect suicidal communication.* The individual uses phrases that do not hint at suicide intentions overtly but the message is implicit all the same: 'We may not see each other again', 'I would like to be remembered as a person who, in spite of all, was not bad', 'Do not worry; I will not disturb you any more.'

- *Non-verbal indirect suicidal communication.* In this case the individual's acts do not hint at the likelihood of an impending suicide but at a premature death. Common manifestations are making a will, planning a funeral, and having preference for topics related to suicide.

**Suicidal crisis** is a crisis in which, when the individual's coping strategies do not work any more, suicide intentions emerge and the person considers the possibility of death for solving – or trying to solve – his problems. This type of crisis requires an appropriate management of time, and the therapist should be directive in trying to keep the person alive, which is the main goal as a duty of care. The duration of the crisis may be variable – it may last hours, days or, rarely, weeks. It can be resolved if the person is able to achieve a better adaptation to life. Otherwise, new crises are likely to appear and, consequently, a suicidal act may occur.

**Suicidal gesture** refers to a suicidal threat based on the suicidal means available but that does not lead to suicide. Suicide attempts without significant physical harm are often seen as gestures. The concept can be misleading as a gesture may not be taken seriously but, nevertheless, be the beginning of a pattern of suicidal behaviours and an indicator of unrelieved distress.

**Suicidal ideation** refers to thoughts about suicide. These may be detailed and planned without ending as a completed suicide. There is a variety of ideas:

- *Wish to die.* A first step that indicates the individual's dissatisfaction with his way of living, a door to suicide ideation. Common expressions in this case are: 'Life is not worth living', 'It is better to be dead than to live this way'.

- *Suicidal representation.* Characterized by passive suicidal fantasies; for instance, the individual visualizes himself hanged.

- *Suicidal idea without a specific method.* The individual expresses his wish to end his life, but when asked how he would do it, he replies that it could be in any way but expresses no preference for any method in particular: by hanging himself, by setting himself on fire, by shooting himself, by jumping from a high place, etc.

- *Suicidal idea with a specific method but without any plan.* The individual expresses his suicidal intentions using a specific method but does not have an elaborate plan.

- *Planned suicidal idea or suicidal plan.* The individual knows *how, when, where, why* and *what for* he will carry out the suicidal act and, as a rule, takes precautions not to be found.

**Suicidal intention** is a deliberate wish by an individual to commit suicide combined with a determination to die. This is often related to suicide risk in terms of the likelihood that the person will complete the act.

**Suicidal logic** refers to the characteristics that make up the suicidal individual's way of thinking – for instance, an urgency to put an end to the unbearable psychache they suffer from due to frustration, psychological needs, anguish, hopelessness, impotence, abandonment, incapacity to find non-suicidal alternatives, or rescue fantasies. It shares many characteristics with pre-suicidal syndromes.

**Suicidal notes** or farewell notes are written and left by suicidal people to express their moods, opinions, wish to die, relationships with significant others, and possible motives. Suicidal notes are not considered as valuable as spoken communications and their importance has been undervalued when seeking information about the suicidal person.

**Suicidal pact** is an agreement between two or more people to die together in the same place and by the same method. It occurs frequently in couples with strong affective bonds, as in the case of spouses, relatives and members of the same political organization or religious sect.

**Suicidal past history** comprises the previous suicidal attempts carried out by the person. This term can also be used to refer to the person's relatives who have had a similar history.

**Suicidal people** are those who have attempted to end their lives recently or in the previous year, those with persistent suicidal ideas and those at risk of committing suicide in the immediate or near future.

**Suicidal plan** comprises suicidal ideas that are logically structured. They are very hazardous because the meaning they convey is that the individual wishes to die using a specific method at a given time for a concrete motive and has taken the necessary precautions not to be stopped.

**Suicidal potential** is a group of suicidal risk factors that are present in an individual who at a certain time can predispose, precipitate or perpetuate a self-destructive behaviour.

**Suicidal process** comprises the time elapsed from the individual's first planned suicidal thought to the moment he makes the suicide attempt. The term emphasizes the development of the event through time, suggesting that suicide is not an act that occurs as a result of an individual's single impulse, but a process that has a history.

**Suicidal profile** comprises the psychological features that best characterize a potential suicidal person such as impulsivity, poor interpersonal relationships and hostility. These are the most frequent features, but not the only ones. There is no single profile common to all suicidal individuals.

**Suicidal risk** refers to people at risk of committing a suicidal act in the immediate future or those who might commit it during their lifetime.

**Suicidal risk groups** are groups of people that exhibit particular risk factors recognized from healthcare research.

**Suicidal situation** is a situation that favours the appearance of high suicidal risk, as in the case of an individual who has had a previous suicide attempt and suffers from depression at present.

**Suicidal tendencies** are the attitudes characterized by the intention, planning and decision or impulse to commit suicide as gleaned from previous or current behaviour.

**Suicidal threats** are spoken or written expressions used to communicate that an individual wishes to die or is about to engage in a suicidal act.

**Suicide** is generally described as the act of taking one's own life on purpose – namely, a lethal outcome that is self-inflicted with the intended goal of dying. There are, however, a variety of definitions of suicide. What most definitions have in common are death as an outcome, the self as agent, an intention to die to achieve a different status and an awareness of the intended outcome. The classification is sometimes questionable, as coroners' reports sometimes attribute accidental death.

**Suicide behaviour** is any action that could cause a person to die, such as taking a drug overdose or crashing a car on purpose.

**Suicide delay** is a pact proposed by a therapist to a person at high suicide risk, who is still capable of establishing an adequate therapist–patient relationship, to postpone the suicide act for a few weeks to allow medication to work and for suicide ideation to disappear. Suicide delays should not be confused with no-suicide contracts, which seek the individual's commitment not to harm himself. In suicide delay the therapist just invites the individual to postpone the suicidal act, not to give it up.

**Suicide incitement** is the name given to the act of encouraging others to commit suicide. Incitement is prosecuted by the law in several countries and goes against the duty of care for the other that most citizens have.

**Suicide prevention** comprises measures used to prevent the occurrence of suicidal acts. It is classified as primary, secondary and tertiary prevention. It can also be categorized as prevention, intervention and postvention, or direct, indirect and general prevention:

- *Direct prevention.* A group of measures that help to abort or resolve a suicidal process by means of non-self-destructive solutions.

- *Indirect prevention.* A group of measures that aim at treating mental and behavioural disorders, or physical conditions, that may lead to suicide and crisis situations, as well as reducing access to the methods by which people can harm themselves, etc.

- *General prevention.* A group of psychological, social and institutional supportive measures that tend to empower citizens to manage vital psycho-traumatic events and mitigate the harm they might cause.

**Suicide prevention strategies** are ways of conducting suicide prevention. There are national and local strategies. The World Health Organization has suggested six major actions to decrease deaths by suicide: treatment of mental diseases, control over the possession of firearms, detoxification of domestic and motor vehicle gases, control over the availability of toxic substances, and restriction of sensationalist news in the mass media.

**Suicide protective factors** are factors that tend to reduce the occurrence of suicidal acts in some individuals – for instance, the support received during a crisis, the management of pain in a terminal disease, the treatment of depressive disorders, an adequate capacity to solve problems, a reasonable level of self-esteem and self-sufficiency, and the capacity to seek help from competent people.

**Suicide rate** is the number of suicides per 100,000 inhabitants that occur in a place each year. It may refer to the whole population or to a specific part of it, according to age or sex groups.

**Suicide typologies** are classifications of suicidal people according to common characteristics. Pérez classifies them according to a person's capacity to take responsibility for their own lives: fully responsible, partially responsible and not responsible. A specific therapeutic relationship should be established for each type during a suicidal crisis (mutual participation, guided and active-passive cooperation respectively).

**Suicidology** is the scientific study of suicidal behaviour, suicide prevention, intervention and rehabilitation. It comprises the study of suicidal thoughts, suicide attempts, and suicide and its prevention.

**Survivors** are persons who have an affective bond to a person who has died by suicide; these include relatives, friends, the physician who assisted the suicide and work colleagues.

*Suttee* (also known as *sati*) is a method linked to the myth of the Hindu goddess Sati who burned herself to death in a fire after her father insulted her husband, the god Shiva. It was common in certain parts of India where a Hindu wife immolated herself on her dead husband's funeral pyre, either voluntarily or by coercion.

**Unavoidable suicides** are suicides committed by people whose clinical characteristics did not allow their physicians to diagnose the impending suicidal hazard.

**Volunteers** is a term applied to members of Befrienders International or the Samaritans, which are suicide prevention organizations. Their work consists of listening and establishing a neutral but affirmative relationship. The Samaritans movement was started by Chad Varah in London in 1953. Befrienders International is based on the experience of this original movement and was founded in November 1974. It is a powerful volunteer organization for suicide prevention present in more than 40 countries from all continents. A volunteer can be a taxi driver, a police officer, a student, a barber, a housewife, a business person, a retired person, or anyone capable of recognizing pre-suicidal symptoms and doing something timely.

**Vulnerable groups** are groups of individuals who, according to their condition, are more likely to commit suicide than the rest of the population. Among them are the elderly, people who live alone, immigrants, native minorities or indigenous peoples, prisoners, and alcohol and substance abusers. Vulnerable groups may also be groups at risk.

**Warning signs** include suicidal or self-destructive thoughts, death ideas, writings about death, sudden changes in an individual's behaviour or sleep or feeding patterns, academic results and feelings of guilt. These signs refer to short-term risks for suicide and need to be understood in context.

**World Suicidology Network** is an organization founded by Professor Sergio A. Pérez Barrero MD. It was formerly known as the Iberoamerican Network of Suicidology, which brought together people interested in suicide prevention, professionals and lay persons, from Iberoamerica and further afield. The main aim of this network is to keep its membership in contact through electronic mail to exchange experiences that might contribute to diminishing this avoidable cause of death. While membership started with colleagues located in the southern hemisphere, plus Spain and Portugal, colleagues from other latitudes also joined the network and it became what is now the World Suicidology Network.

# REFERENCES

Aldridge, D. (1998) *Suicide: The Tragedy of Hopelessness*. London: Jessica Kingsley Publishers.

Cavanagh, J. Carson, A., Sharpe, M. and Lawrie, S. (2003) 'Psychological autopsy studies of suicide: a systematic review.' *Psychological Medicine 33*, 3: 395–405.

Deisenhammer, E.A., Huber, M., Kemmler, G., Weiss, E.M. and Hinterhuber, H. (2007) 'Suicide victims' contacts with physicians during the year before death.' *European Archives of Psychiatry and Clinical Neuroscience 257*, 8: 480–485.

Hawton, K. and van Heeringen, K. (2009) 'Suicide.' *The Lancet 373*, 9672: 1372–1381.

Moran, P. Coffey, C., Romaniuk, H. *et al.* (2011) 'The natural history of self-harm from adolescence to young adulthood: a population-based cohort study.' *The Lancet.* doi:10.1016/S0140-6736(11)61141-0.

National Institute of Mental Health (2010) 'Suicide in the U.S.: Statistics and Prevention.' Available at www.nimh.nih.gov/health/publications/suicide-in-the-us-statistics-and-prevention/index.shtml#suicide-attempts, accessed on 16 January 2012.

Schneidman, E. (1993) *Suicide as Psychache: A Clinical Approach to Self-destructive Behaviour.* New York: Jason Aronson.

# FURTHER INFORMATION

## USEFUL READING

Hawton, K. (2005) *Prevention and Treatment of Suicidal Behaviour: From Science to Practice.* Oxford: Oxford University Press.

Hawton, K., Rodham, K. and Evans, E. (2006) *By Their Own Young Hand. Deliberate Self-harm and Suicidal Ideas in Adolescents.* London: Jessica Kingsley Publishers.

Hawton, K. and van Herringen, K. (2002) *The International Handbook of Suicide and Attempted Suicide.* Oxford: Wiley.

Pérez Barrero, S. (2007) 'Suicide prevention: A resource for the family.' *Iranian Journal of Psychiatry and Behavioral Sciences (IJPBS)* 1, 2, Autumn and Winter. Available at www.sid.ir/en/VEWSSID/J_pdf/118620080201.pdf, accessed on 22 November 2011.

Suicide.org (2012) 'International Suicide Statistics.' Available at www.suicide.org/international-suicide-statistics.html, accessed on 16 January 2012.

SUPRE (2000) *Preventing Suicide: A Resource for Media Professionals.* Geneva: World Health Organization. Available at www.who.int/mental_health/media/en/426.pdf, accessed on 22 November 2011.

Wasserman, D. and Wasserman, C. (2009) *Oxford Textbook of Suicidology and Suicide Prevention. A Global Perspective.* Oxford: Oxford University Press.

## WEBSITES

**European Network for Suicidology**
A cooperative network for people working full-time or part-time (or professionally or voluntarily) with the problem of suicidal behaviour.
*www.uke.de/extern/ens*

### International Association for Suicide Prevention (IASP)
An international association concerned with the study and prevention of suicide.
*www.iasp.info*

### QPR Institute
An online resource, QPR stands for Question, Persuade and Refer, offering to train people how to recognize the warning signs of a suicide crisis and refer someone for help.
*www.qprinstitute.com/index.html*

### Suicide Prevention Resource Center
An organization dedicated to promote and disseminate strategies for suicide prevention.
*www.sprc.org/about_sprc/partners.asp*

### WHO
The World Health Organization has a suicide prevention website (SUPRE) with a broad spectrum of information about suicide and mental health.
www.who.int/mental_health/prevention/suicide/suicideprevent/en

### World Suicidology Net / Red Mundial de Suicidiólogos RMS
World Suicidology Net gathers people and organizations via email who are interested in suicide prevention. Members of the organization come from any country of the world. The headquarters is in Bayamo, Cuba.
*http://es-la.facebook.com/pages/Red-Mundial-de-Suicidologos-ONG/160812213964281?sk=info*

# INDEX

Page numbers in *italics* refer to figures

Abimelech 26
Absalom 27
academic problems 61
accidental suicide 45–6, 161
acute stressors 161, 163
adolescents 55, 62, 69, 98–9, 101, 112, 113
    alcohol consumption 121
    bullying 70–1, 150
    depression 92, 120, 150
    factors in suicide 74–5, 91–2, 120
    familial situation 120
    hospitalization 124–5
    parent-child relationship 88–9
    personal situation 120
    substance abuse 93, 121
    suicidal crisis 119–21
    suicidal crisis therapy 121–5
    survivors 133
aggression 70, 71, 72, 86, 92, 153
    adolescents 120
    children 117
    impulsive aggression 89
Ahithopel 27
Ajax 23
alcohol abuse 12, 15, 38, 51, 63, 68, 72–3, 82, 133, 146, 147, 148, 149, 155, 158, 160
    elderly people 129, 130
    impact on families 86–7
alcohol consumption 56, 60, 65, 87, 92, 114, 121
Aldridge, D. 13–17, 52, 53, 68, 156
alienation 80, 153, 162
altruistic suicide 28, 161

ambivalence 43, 50, 114, 126, 138
American Psychiatric Association (APA) 66
Amicus 23
amplified suicide 161
anger 30, 98–9
anguish 59, 60, 66, 121, 151, 169, 174
anomic suicide 162
Antiochus Epiphanes 28
antisocial behaviour 71, 88, 91, 92, 153, 163
anxiety 20, 38, 60, 91, 158
apparent suicide 162
art 22, 23–4, 25, 31, 32
Asia 55
assisted suicide 20, 25, 44, 82–3
    doctor-assisted suicide 20, 47–8, 83
    EXIT 47, 83
    impact on others 33
attempted suicide 12, 15, 63, 67–8, 172
    definition 37–9
    intention to die 41–2
    myths 50, 54
Australia 20, 138
    Australian Aboriginals 82

bad news 58, 61
Bathsheba 27
Befrienders International 178
Belgium 20
bereavement 63, 107
Biblical suicides 26–31
biological theory 162–3
bipolar disorder 38, 47
blackmail suicide 43–4, 49
blame 95, 97–8
bleeding 163
bluff 49, 50, 122

bravery 54
Browne, Sir Thomas *Religion of a Physician* 32
bullying 26, 62, 68, 70–1, 91, 150
    cyberbullying 70, 71, 138, 139, 143, 150, 164

calls for help 38, 45, 99
Canace 23–4
cancer 20, 60
carbon monoxide inhalation 39
carers 106, 107, 112, 163
Cato 32
Cavanagh, J. 92
Centre for Suicide Prevention 163
change of status 112–13
chat rooms 138
Chatterton, Thomas 31–2
children 55, 101, 113
    borderline personality disorder 93–4
    bullying 70–1, 91, 150
    child mental health 91–4
    child neglect 89–90
    concept of death 117
    factors in suicide 74
    hospitalization 119
    maternal depression 85–6
    parent-child relationship 88–9
    parental suicide 103–4
    sexual identity 90–1
    suicidal crisis 117–19
    survivors 133
China 55
Christianity 32
chronic stressors 163–4
chronic suicidal behaviours 163–4
classification 37
    accidental suicide 45–6
    clinical manifestation 43–4
    intention to die 41–2
    methods of suicide 39–41
    ranking methods 42–3
    suicidal ideation 44–5
    suicidal threats 45
    suicide or an attempt? 37–9
    unavoidable suicides 46–8
Cleopatra 24

Collatinus 25
collective suicides 140–1
communication 12, 13, 137
community of intimates 13, 107, 112, 142
competence 16
conflicts 11, 12, 16
    avoidance of conflict 79
    *see also* familial conflicts
coping mechanisms 20, 42, 98, 99
    alcohol 15, 129
    repertoire of distress management 170
    substance abuse 93
counselling 113–14
    psychological first aid 114–17
    stages of psychological first aid *115*
counsellors 16, 83, 100, 109, 110
courage 54
court cases 58, 61
cowardice 54
crying 56, 60, 92, 121
Cuba 28, 165, 170
    National Program for the Prevention of Suicide 151
cultural influences 12, 22–5, 26, 63, 67, 75
    loss of culture 82
cutting oneself 40
cyberbullying 70, 71, 138, 139, 143, 150, 164
cybersuicide 138, 141, 164

David 27
David, Jacques-Louis *The Death of Socrates* 32
death 15, 19–21, 22, 61, 113–14, 152
Deisenhammer, E.A. 129
delinquency 16, 158, 159
delusions 46–7
dementia 47, 64, 65, 67
Demetrius 29
Demosthenes 25
depression 12, 38, 51, 63, 68, 136, 146, 147, 149, 158
    adolescents 92, 120, 150
    alcohol abuse 72
    Australian Aboriginals 82
    bipolar disorder 47
    depression as abnormal ageing 65
    depression as mental illness 66–7

depression related to organic complaints 66
elderly people 64–7, 130, 131, 150
maternal depression 85–6
Desfontaine, Abbot 33
desperate suicide 43
deviance 12, 14, 16, 33, 71, 94
disorders 164
disorders *see* bipolar disorder; mood disorders; personality disorders; post-traumatic stress disorder
distress 13–17, 68, 95, 152
alcohol abuse 72, 73, 87
assisted suicide 83
escalating distress *14*
familial distress 85, 89, 94, 104, 111, 135, 155–60
negotiating distress 135–6
risk factors associated with suicide *76*
survivors 98–9
distress management 16, 17, 20, 42, 52, 119, 151, 155–60
levels of escalating distress and systemic strategies of management *157*
limited repertoire 121, 124, 133
repertoire of distress management 170
divorce 15, 63, 67, 112
doctors 13, 32, 42, 73, 109, 133, 149, 151, 169
'doctor shopping' 129
doctor-assisted suicide 20, 47–8, 83
suicidal behaviour in medical profession 136
double suicide 164
drowning 165
Durkheim, Émile 37
dying 20

educational initiatives 149–50
egoistic suicide 165
Elah 27
elderly people 47, 48, 55, 112, 113, 146
abuse 132
depressed elderly people 64–7
factors in suicide 75–6, 130
suicidal crisis 129–32
Eleazar 28

employment 68
'end of life decisions' 20
England 32, 141–2, 146–7
ethnic minorities 73–4, 147
Europe 34
euthanasia 20, 25, 26, 44, 82–3
EXIT 47, 83, 88
exsanguination 24, 163
extended suicide 161

factories 52
factors in suicide 63, 67–8, 69
acute stressors 161, 163
chronic stressors 163
elderly people 75–6, 130
protective factors 79, *80*, 177
risk factors *76*, 170
situational factors 73–7
familial conflicts 12, 54, 68, 85, 95, 155, 158
alcohol abuse 86–7
child mental health 91–4
child neglect 89–90
parent-child relationship 88–9
parental mental health 85–6
personality disorders 87–8
sexual identity 90–1
familial distress 85, 89, 94, 104, 111, 135, 155–60
families 12, 13, 15–16, 106–7, 118–19, 152–3
adolescents 122, 123
family counselling 131–2
Internet 142
mutual rejection 113
farewell notes 56, 61, 118, 121, 172, 174
farmers 51, 52, 81, 152
fatalistic suicide 165
fear 60, 99, 100
fear suicide 43
Fielding, Henry 20
financial problems 12, 31, 65, 68, 130
fire 27, 28, 165
firearms 21, 38, 129, 145, 147, 165, 170, 172
*folie à deux* 141
France 33

friends 16, 106, 122, 123, 153
frustrated suicide 165

gender 38, 63, 67
general practitioners 15, 16, 111, 129, 136, 146, 147, 158
genetic influences 51–2
Geneva, Switzerland 21–2
Goethe, Johann Wolfgang von *The Sorrows of Young Werther* 32
Greece, ancient 22, 23, 25
grief 83, 97, 165
  complicated grief 101–3
  physical symptoms 100
  signs and symptoms *102*
guilt 97–8

hallucinations 46
hanging 38, 39, 129, 165
Hannibal 23
*hara-kiri* 23, 166, 172
harassment 62, 70, 74
Hawton, K. 138, 146
health problems 65, 66
healthcare professionals 106, 107, 146, 147
historical suicides 21–5
homicide, extended 26, 47, 53–4
homosexuality 68, 90
honour 23, 25, 30, 34
Hope Telephone 166
hopelessness 52, 54, 56, 61, 65, 68, 72, 74, 77
  carers 112
  counselling 113
  cultural factors 87
humiliation 27, 61, 71, 74, 118, 167
hypersomnia 92

iatrogenesis 160, 166
Iberoamerican Network of Suicidology 179
identity 23, 25
illness 58, 61, 69
  terminal illness 47
immigrants 73–4, 147, 179
immolation 28, 165, 170, 171
impulsive suicide 52

impulsivity 52, 72, 86, 87, 88, 93, 94, 121, 175
India 28, 165, 170, 178
  suicide among farmers 51, 52, 152
indigenous peoples 82, 86, 87, 148, 179
*inseki-jisatsu* 166
intentionality 32, 33, 41–2, 46, 49, 166, 169, 174
interagency initiatives 149
international initiatives 145–8
Internet 16, 70, 71, 137–8
  coalition of the disaffected 139–40
  suicide pacts 139–40, 140–3
intervention techniques 126–7
  differing therapeutic relationships *128–9*
intimates 136
  community of intimates 13, 107, 112, 142
Islam 55
isolation 33, 51, 53, 65, 71, 87, 98

Japan 23, 34, 140, 166
Jesus 30
Judas Iscariot 30
Judas Maccabeus 29
jumping 38, 46, 166

*karojisatsu* 166
Krien, Gerald 140

Latin America 55
lethality of method 39, 166–7
  harmless methods 39
  hazardous non-lethal methods 40
  hazardous potentially lethal methods 40
  lethal methods 40
life 20–1
listening 53, 113
literature 24, 25, 31, 32, 33
London, England 141–2
loneliness 65, 93, 100, 120, 121, 126, 127
loss 15, 21, 22, 61, 65, 75, 77
  assisted suicide 83
  loss of culture 82
  substance abusers 93
  survivors 98–9, 134

Louvre Museum, Paris 23
Lucretia 25

Macareus 23
manipulation 49, 94, 112, 117, 118, 122
Mark Anthony 24
Márques, Gabriel Garciá 12
marriage 21–2, 63
martyrdom 22, 30, 34, 51
mass media 55–6, 138, 146, 147, 148, 151
mass suicide 167
Mayans 22
meaning 62, 135, 167
medication 15, 16, 65, 114, 124, 131
mental health provision 81–2
mental illness 12, 51, 66–7, 68, 69, 77,
    130, 138, 146, 147, 148
    parents 85–6
messages of intent 12, 114, 172–3
methods of suicide 39, 57, 167
    lethality 39–40, 50
    ranking methods 42–3
    significance 40–1
Metropolitan Museum of Art, New York 32
Mexico 22
Middle East 141
military personnel 104
Montana-Wyoming Tribal Leaders
    Association 148
mood disorders 38, 47, 51, 63, 72, 86, 91
Moran, P. 67
motive 61–2, 167
mythology 22
myths 49–56, 168

national initiatives 145–8
National Institute of Mental Health (NIMH)
    38
Nero 24
Netherlands 20, 47–8
Nicanor 29
no-suicide contracts 122, 124, 168, 176
Northern Ireland 30
Norway 147

oblation 168
Octavia 24

Odysseus 23
overdosing 39, 40, 93, 112–13, 129, 160
Ovid *Pyramus and Thisbe* 32

pain 20, 111, 132, 134, 151, 158, 160
    change of status 112–13
    pain management 82–3, 123–4
palliative care 20, 44, 82, 124, 162
panic attacks 15
parasomnia pseudosuicide 169
parasuicide 45, 168, 172
parents 90–1, 100, 118, 123, 153
    mental health 85–8
    parent-child relationship 88–9
passive suicide 130
pathology 16
Pérez Barrero, S. 126, 128, 153, 177, 179
personal characteristics 79
personal responsibility 125–7
    differing therapeutic relationships *128–9*
personality disorders 38, 47, 68, 87–8
    children 93–4
pesticides 40, 81, 145, 146, 147, 152, 170
Peter 30
Peterson, Jeret 'Speedy' 102–3
Philometer 28
planned suicide 12, 34, 45, 57, 62, 122–3,
    175
poetry 19
poisoning 28, 31
    agricultural substances 39, 40, 81, 146,
    147
Pompeia 24
Portugal 179
post-traumatic stress disorder 104, 133
postvention 168, 177
poverty 54, 148, 152
pre-suicidal syndrome 52, 119, 168, 174,
    178
prevention 49, 145, 151–3, 176–7
    community initiatives 150
    comprehensive national programme
    149–51
    Cuban National Program for the
    Prevention of Suicide 151
    educational initiatives 149–50
    indigenous peoples 148

prevention *cont.*
  interagency initiatives 149
  international and national initiatives
    145–8
  media initiatives 151
  myths about suicide 49–56
Prevost, Abbot *Manon Lescaut* 33
prisoners 45–6, 75, 165, 179
problem resolution 16
protective factors 79, *80*, 177
  social problems 81–2
pseudosuicide 168–9
psychache 169, 174
psychiatric institutions 41, 52
psychiatrists 13, 53, 73, 97, 100, 111, 112,
    129, 149
psychological autopsy 63, 92, 169
psychological first aid 114–17, 165
  stages *115*
psychologists 13, 71, 100, 112, 149
psychotherapy *see* therapy
Ptolemy Macron 28, 29
'putting things in order' 27

rational suicide 34, 169–70
Razis 29–30
rejection 50, 98, 113, 123
  parental rejection 88, 89, 90
relationships 12, 15, 16–17, 68
  break-ups 61
  death 61
  parent-child relationship 88–9, 142
  personality disorders 87–8
relatives of a suicide 12
relief 100
remorse 30, 33, 85, 87, 166
repeaters 47, 60, 170
resilience 82, 151, 160
resources 16
responsibility 125–7, 128–9, 134–5, 153
retirement 63
revenge 23, 26, 27, 30, 43–4, 62
reward 42
  reward in Paradise 22
risk factors *76*, 170
risk groups 56, 63–4, 175
  alcohol abusers 72–3
  depressed elderly people 64–7

previous suicide attempts 67–8
  situational factors 73–7
  survivors 73
  threats of suicide 69
  vulnerable people in crisis 69–71
Rome, ancient 23–4
Royal Academy of the Spanish Language 33

sacrifice suicide 44
Samaritans 13, 171, 178
Samson 26, 28
Sands, Bobby 30
*sati see suttee*
Saul 26
schizophrenia 38, 47, 51, 120–1, 126
school shootings 26, 53
  Colombine 70–1, 139
self-blame 73, 98
self-destructive behaviour 42, 44, 118, 163,
    171, 175
self-esteem 28
self-harm 43, 45, 61, 82, 164, 168, 171
  deliberate self-harm syndrome 164
self-help groups 150, 171
self-inflicted harm 37, 46, 94, 171
self-injury 68
self-mutilation 45, 171
self-starvation 30, 34, 171–2
self-worth 54
Seneca 24
separation 15, 63, 67, 112
*seppuku* 23, 166, 172
sexual abuse 87, 103
Shakespeare, William *Romeo and Juliet* 32
shame 23–4, 25, 33, 34
Shneidman, Edwin *Suicide as Psychache* 169
shooting oneself 39, 40
siblings 103–4
significance of methods 40–1
significant others 13, 16, 33, 52, 74, 174
  bullying 70
  impact of suicide 73, 98–9, 100
sisters 141
social interaction 65, 79
social workers 13, 106, 158
socio-political problems 54
Socrates 25
Soviet bloc 55

Spain 23, 179
specialist help 15
spousal conflicts 12
Sri Lanka 28, 165, 170
statistics 11, 170
stigma 50, 77, 81, 99, 102, 113, 132, 148, 150, 165
substance abuse 38, 51, 63, 68, 82, 92, 133, 146, 147, 148, 155, 157, 158, 160
suffering 20, 54, 82–3, 113, 124, 151
suicidal circumstances 40–1, 172
suicidal communications 12, 13, 172–3
suicidal crisis 13, 30–1, 46, 50, 55, 173
  adolescents 119–25
  adults 125–7
  children 117–19
  elderly people 129–32
  questions to ask 105–10
  relationships 106–7, 110
  signs of crisis 56
  warning signs 111–13, 179
suicidal gestures 42, 43, 45, 49, 99, 125, 173
suicidal ideation 38–9, 44–5, 58, 173–4, 176
  alcohol abuse 68, 73, 87
  approaching the topic 58–9
  children 90
  elderly people 64
  hints and suspicions 59–62
  plans and methods 57
suicidal logic 129, 174
suicidal notes 56, 61, 118, 121, 172, 174
suicidal pacts 139–40, 140–3, 174
suicidal past history 68, 91, 114, 135, 175
suicidal profile 175
suicide 11–13, 176
  attitudes towards suicide 162
  biological theory 162–3
  first use of term 32–3
  genetic influences 51–2
  intentional act 33, 41–2, 166, 174
  myths about suicide 49–56
  narrative structure 30–1
suicide bombers 22, 26, 34, 53–4
  compared to individual suicides 35
suicide by cop 172
suicide delay 176

suicide incitement 139–40, 140, 141, 142, 143, 164, 176
suicide typologies 177–8
suicidology 56, 92, 169–70, 178, 179
survivors 73, 97, 105, 146, 178
  adolescents 133
  anger 98–9, 133, 134
  assisted suicide 83, 133
  blame 97–8
  children 133
  complicated grief 101–3, 133
  grief 99–101, 133
  guilt 97–8, 133, 134–5
  helping survivors 132–5
  imitation 135
  loss 98–9, 134
  siblings and suicide 103–4
suttee 28, 165, 178
Sweden 20, 147
Switzerland 20, 47, 88

talking about suicide 52–3, 56, 69, 127
  approaching the topic 58–9
  asking about motives 61–2
  asking about plans 60–1
  hints and suspicions 59–60
Tarquinius 25
teenagers see adolescents
television 41, 117, 147, 151
Thatcher, Margaret 30
therapists 100–1, 114, 130–1, 153
therapy 16, 105, 106, 118
  therapeutic relationships 128–9
threats of suicide 12, 45, 49, 56, 69, 176
toxic substances 146, 147

unavoidable suicides 46–8, 178
unemployment 54, 63, 75, 86, 152
  ex-service personnel 104
United States of America 20, 38, 48, 139, 140, 165, 170

van Heeringen, K. 138, 146
Varah, Chad 178
violence 69, 73, 74, 86, 93, 148, 170
volunteers 178
vulnerable people 12, 69–71, 178–9

warning signs 179
  change of status 112–13
  escalation of symptoms 111
  familial conflict 111
  frequency of consultations 111
  hopelessness 112
  mutual rejection 113
  someone leaves or is about to leave 112
wealth 54–5
websites 138
widowed people 21, 28, 55, 75, 165
will-making 61
withdrawal 65, 72, 87, 92, 99, 120, 159
World Health Organization 11, 46, 146,
  177
World Suicidology Network 179

Zimri 27